HOMOSEXUALITY
and the
MAGISTERIUM

HOMOSEXUALITY
and the
MAGISTERIUM

Documents from the Vatican and U.S. Bishops 1975 - 1985

edited by
John Gallagher

NEW WAYS MINISTRY
Mt. Rainier, Maryland

Acknowledgments

The editor and publisher are grateful to the USCC and the bishops whose documents are contained herein.

Excerpt from *A Challenge to Love* edited by Robert Nugent, copyright 1983 by New Ways Ministry, reprinted with permission of the Crossroad Publishing Company, New York.

Excerpt from *To Live in Christ Jesus*, copyright by the United States Catholic Conference and used with permission.

''Who Is Our Neighbor?'' reprinted from *All God's People* by Rembert Weakland, O.S.B. Copyright 1985 by Rembert Weakland and used with permission of Paulist Press.

Library of Congress Catalog Number
85-61818
ISBN 0-935877-00-2

New Ways Ministry
4012 29th St.
Mt. Rainier, MD 20712
Second Printing, 1988

...the Church can combat the evil of prejudice against homosexuals by strongly proclaiming the gross evil of prejudicial attitudes and conduct toward lesbians and gays; by fostering legislation at all levels in the State and in the ecclesiastical arena to remove systemic prejudice; by making efforts to purify of all prejudice the manner in which it conveys its moral teaching on homosexuality; by encouraging empirical research on homosexuality and the ways to combat prejudice against lesbians and gays, and by fostering ongoing theological research and criticism, with regard to its own theological tradition on homosexuality, none of which is infallibly taught.

Washington State
Catholic Conference
April 28, 1983

CONTENTS

INTRODUCTION

The Senate of Priests of the Archdiocese of San Francisco say that any effective plan for a ministry to homosexual people "must be based upon the teachings of the Church, the results of modern social sciences and the real lived experiences of homosexual men and women." (1)

Too often the "teachings" of the Church on homosexuality have been collapsed to a simplistic, unnuanced and, at times, even unfeeling reiteration of the condemnation of homogenital behavior. Too often Church "teachings" on this complex and emotional subject that affects the lives of millions of Catholics throughout the world either directly or through families, relatives or friends has proven to be a cold, hard stone rather than warm, nourshing bread. Too often the equally central "moral teaching" on justice for homosexual citizens, sensitive pastoral care for gay and lesbian Christians, the serious obligation of the Church to name and eliminate prejudice and discrimination from its own life and the fundamental dignity of each human person which is the theme of the current papacy are either ignored, minimized or often even totally unknown.

One of the main purposes of this collection of magisterial statements on homosexuality is to bring together for the first time in one place documentation that can easily be read, analyzed and compared as part of "the teachings of the Church." As any casual reader of these documents will readily recognize these teachings go far beyond a prohibition of same-sex expression. While a complete picture of Church teaching on homosexuality must include and deal with this dimension, we can neither begin nor end with this particular aspect if we wish to do justice both to Church teachings and homosexual Christians. All of the documents in this collection repeat in a variety of ways and with different emphases, the magisterial teaching on homogenital expression in an objective sense. Most of them, however, also attempt to consider subjective factors which touch the lives of people who experience in themselves a homosexual identity such as their basic human needs for friendship, acceptance and affirmation. These documents, for the most part, are conscious of the warning from a British statement which says that "Pastoral care does not consist simply in the rigid and automatic application of objective moral norms . . . while the objective norms are clear-cut, the application of such norms may be complicated."(2)

The articulation of magisterial teaching on homogenital behavior is not the main point of most of these statements from Roman and United States Catholic sources. With but few exceptions they all make some attempt to take seriously the words of Bishop Walter Sullivan. Once we have clearly articulated the official position on homosexuality, said Sullivan, "we cannot remain satisfied that nothing else remains to be done in the area of pastoral care for homosexual people and education on the topic for the larger human community, including the families and friends of homosexual people.'' (3)

Many of the contributions to *Homosexuality and the Magisterium* also evidence some awareness that the simple and unnuanced repetition of magisterial teaching on homogenital behavior can, itself, be a source of oppression for gay and lesbian people. This is true not only for those who remain in the Catholic community, but also for others in our society where the impact of the Church teaching extends far beyond the confines of the Catholic Church. Bishop Sullivan suggests that pastoral care is expecially urgent ''in those cases where the teaching of the Church itself has been presented in such a way that it has been the source or occasion of some of the pain and alienation that many homosexual Catholics experience.''(4) He is not alone in this concern.

The Roman Catholic Bishops of Washington state also admit that many Catholics have given to the Church's teaching a nuance which is prejudicial to homosexual people. ''While the Church's teaching with regard to homosexuality . . . does not by itself cause prejudice . . . it seems true to say that the manner in which Church teaching has been concretely conveyed has contributed to the prejudice against gays and lesbians.'' (5) At times the reason for this prejudicial attitude has been either misunderstanding or misuse of Church teaching. At other times, however, the cause can be found in a one-sided presentation of magisterial teaching which stresses the Church's moral judgment about certain forms of sexual expression while offering only a token concern for the other equally serious and binding teachings on social justice, pastoral ministry and human dignity as they relate to gay and lesbian people. This kind of approach while totally ''orthodox'' in one sense, is still a serious violation of Catholic belief, and in the long run, a much more harmful distortion of ''Church teaching'' than is a presentation which fails to give full and serious consideration to magisterial teaching on homogenital expression.

Not every official statement on homosexuality has been included in this collection. In the past ten years many other statements have appeared both in the United States and abroad. Some of them deal with particular legislation either supporting or opposing ''gay rights.'' Most of these types of statements have been content to repeat magisterial teaching without attempting to develop in any substantial way the pastoral approach to gay and lesbian people. Neither do they make any effort to sort out and clarify the complex issues and apparent conflict of rights usually invovled in legislation as, for example, the Bishops of Massachusetts do in their statement.

We have selected those statements of the past ten years which we feel best convey some sense of movement and growth in the Church's awareness of the reality of a homosexual identity in our Church and culture. One other major document which appeared in 1973 should be recognized although not a part of this anthology.(6) By including the documents we did, however, we do not mean to suggest that we recommend every one of them completely and without, in some cases, serious reservations. We have included at least two because they are examples of the serious confusion in concepts and terminology, a one-sided preoccupation with sexual behaviors, an insensitivity in language and an obvious lack of any serious or prolonged consultation with the real lives and experiences of homosexual Christians.

For the most part we feel that this collection contains statements that embody at least an attempt on the part of some Church leaders to come to a deeper and more sensitive understanding of and appreciation for the experiences of lesbian and gay Catholics. For many readers, however, we know that even these attempts will not be sufficient to meet the challenges and questions that are being raised today among theologians, educators, pastors, therapists and, most especially, among homosexual people of faith. In at least one case a committee of highly competent and dedicated individuals has issued its own report as an alternative to another official pastoral plan.(7)

This collection, then attempts to present a "state of the arts" picture of contemporary magisterial teachings on homosexuality. It is but one more step on a continuing journey in faith to speak the truth in love on the part of those who are commissioned leaders in the Catholic community. It is but one source, although a central one, from which individuals and groups can draw as they confront new situations and challenging questions in their own lives as faithful people with a gay or lesbian identity.

Do these documents speak the last word from the Church on homosexuality? Is there nothing more to be said, no new light to break through, nothing more to be learned, nothing further to explore? For some the answer to these questions, at least substantially, is positive; for others, the answer reflects more the two remarks from the Bishops of Washington state. In their introduction to *Prejudice Against Homosexuals and the Ministry of the Church* the authors assert that since the paper has been commissioned by Church authorities, it represents "an official Church position." (8) They add, however, that the paper "does not attempt to rethink or to develop substantially the Catholic position on the morality of homosexuality — however much such rethinking and development is needed in this and all other areas of the Church's tradition."(9)

The same document later suggests concrete ways in which the Church can combat the evil of prejudice against homosexual people. One way is by "fostering ongoing theological research criticism, with regard to its own theological tradition on homosexuality, none of which is infallibly taught." (10)

Is the "official position" on homosexuality likely to change? One Archbishop answered this question by noting that there are "credible theologians in the church who say it cannot; there are also credible theologians who believe it can."(11) As a Bishop, though, he thought it important for him "to stand clearly within the tradition of the church on this matter."(12)

All of the contributions to *Homosexuality and the Magisterium* stand clearly within the tradition of the church on homosexuality. Yet each of them does so in a slightly different way and some of them are more creative in their attempts to respond to the increasing insistence that the Church engage in serious study, dialogue and ministry on the issue of homosexuality. Fortunately the Church tradition is rich and broad enough to embrace a willingness to continue the search for truth and an openness to the Spirit and to realize that God is always breaking in with new lights for us. That light and truth often come from the most unexpected of quarters including a careful study of magisterial teaching. The Vatican *Declaration on Sexual Ethics* says that "traditional doctrine must be studied more deeply and handed on in a way capable of properly enlightening the consciences of those confronted with new situations . . . it must be enriched with a discernment of all the elements that can truthfully and usefully be brought forward about the meaning and value of human sexuality."(13) Thus, official magisterial teaching itself can be a source of new light and new truths on homosexuality.

Likewise the Church's theological community is another source of new light and truth. John Paul II has said that the Church's social teachings are "by no means closed."(14) On the contrary they are "open to all the new questions which are so numerous today. In this perspective, the contributions of theologians and other thinkers in all parts of the world to the reflection of the Church is indispensable."(15) Can the same be said about teachings on homosexuality?

Cardinal Joseph Ratzinger, in speaking of the work of moral theologians, told some 250 Bishops in 1984 that "the task of the moral theologians is not simply being in service to the teaching office."(16) The moral theologian, Ratzinger said, "Will also take up the new questions which new developments and relationships pose for the traditional norms."(17) Regarding the magisterium, Ratzinger described the work of the moral theologian, in part, in this way. The theologian "goes before it, noticing new questions, gathering knowledge of the objective content and preparing answers."(18)

It is our hope that this collection will provide pastors, theologians, educators and others including gay and lesbian Christians with a valuable resource for contemporary discussions of homosexuality in the Catholic context. While some will find themselves uncomfortable with some of the attitudes and approaches found in these documents, we hope that all will find in them at least a creative stimulus to engage in and continue to promote the strenuous and energizing tasks of reflection, response, criticism, challenging, dialogue and clarification that are vital elements in the historical dialectic between theologians, the faithful and the episcopal magisterium.

The clarification and development of the Church's response to gay and lesbian Christians is a unique contribution of the U.S. Catholic community to the larger Church. Our pastors, theologians, Bishops and lay peole have spoken and written extensively on this subject more so than any other Catholic community. Hopefully, our labors will hasten that time of justice and compassion and Paul's vision of a community in which there is neither Jew nor Greek, slave or free, male or female and where the barriers of sexual orientation will be breached and the wall of division torn down.

John Gallagher

References

1. Senate of Priests. *Ministry and Homosexuality in the Archdiocese of San Francisco.* San Francisco: Senate of Priests, 1983, p. 3.

2. Catholic Social Welfare Commission. *An Introduction to the Pastoral Care of Homosexual People.* Mt. Rainier: New Ways Ministry, 1981, p. 9.

3. Nugent, R. (Ed.). *A Challenge to Love: Gay and Lesbian Catholics in the Church.* New York: Crossroad, 1983, p. xii.

4. Nugent, *ibid.*

5. Washington State Catholic Conference. *The Prejudice Against Homosexuals and the Ministry of the Church.* Seattle: Washington State Catholic Conference, 1983, p. 6.

6. National Conference of Catholic Bishops. *Guide to Confessors in Questions of Homosexuality.* Washington, D.C.: United States Catholic Conference, 1973.

7. Task Force on Gay/Lesbian Issues. *Homosexuality and Social Justice.* San Francisco: Commission on Social Justice, 1982.

8. Washington State Catholic Conference, *op. cit.,* p. 1.

9. Washington State Catholic Conference, *ibid.*

10. Washington State Catholic Conference, *op. cit.*, p. 9.

11. Hunthausen, R. *Archbishop Addresses Issue of Homosexuality*. Mt. Rainier, MD: *Bondings,* Fall, 1983, p. 1.

12. Hunthausen, *ibid.*

13. Congregation for the Doctrine of the Faith. *Vatican Declaration on Sexual Ethics.* Washington, D.C.: United States Catholic Conference, 1976, p. 15.

14. Sacred Congregation for the Doctrine of the Faith. *Vatican Statement on Liberation Theology*. Kansas City, MO: *National Catholic Reporter,* September 21, 1984, p. 14.

15. Ratzinger, J. ''Sources of Moral Theology.'' *The Priest,* September, 1984, p. 18.

16. Ratzinger, *ibid.*

17. Ratzinger, *ibid.*

18. Ratzinger, *ibid.*

Declaration on Certain Questions Concerning Sexual Ethics

Sacred Congregation for the Doctrine of the Faith

Rome
December 29, 1975

Excerpt

At the present time there are those who, basing themselves on observations in the psychological order, have begun to judge indulgently, and even to excuse completely, homosexual relations between certain people. This they do in opposition to the constant teaching of the Magisterium and to the moral sense of the Christian people.

A distinction is drawn, and it seems with some reason, between homosexuals whose tendency comes from a false education, from a lack of normal sexual development, from habit, from bad example, or from other similar causes, and is transitory or at least not incurable; and homosexuals who are definitively such because of some kind of innate instinct or a pathological constitution judged to be incurable.

In regard to this second category of subjects, some people conclude that their tendency is so natural that it justifies in their case homosexual relations within a sincere communion of life and love analogous to marriage, in so far as such homosexuals feel incapable of enduring a solitary life.

In the pastoral field, those homosexuals must certainly be treated with understanding and sustained in the hope of overcoming their personal difficulties and their inability to fit into society. Their culpability will be judged with prudence. But no pastoral method can be employed which would give moral justification to these acts on the grounds that they would be consonant with the condition of such people. For according to the objective moral order, homosexual relations are acts which lack an essential and indispensable finality. In Sacred Scripture they are condemned as a serious depravity and even presented as the sad consequence of rejecting God. This judgment of Scripture does not of course permit us to conclude that all those who suffer from this anomaly are personally responsible for it, but it does attest to the fact that homosexual acts are intrinsically disordered and can in no case be approved.

Sexuality - God's Gift

Bishop Francis Mugavero
Brooklyn, New York

February 11, 1976

Excerpt

The complexus of anthropological, psychological and theological reasoning in regard to human sexuality has contributed to the Church's teaching that heterosexuality is normative. All should strive for a sexual integration which respects that norm since any other orientation respects less adequately the full spectrum of human relationships.

Whatever the cause of the homosexual orientation, both to those who share that orientation and to society in general, there are certain cautions we wish to put forward.

We urge homosexual men and women to avoid identifying their personhood with their sexual orientation. They are so much more as persons than this single aspect of their personality. That richness must not be lost.

Being subject to misunderstanding and at times unjust discrimination has resulted in an overreaction on the part of some persons of homosexual orientation. It is not homosexuality which should be one's claim to acceptance or human rights or to being loved by us all; it is the fact that we are all brothers and sisters under the Fatherhood of God. Our community must explore ways to secure the legitimate rights of all our citizens, regardless of sexual orientation, while being sensitive to the understanding and hopes of all involved.

On a more personal level, we wish to express our concern and compassion for those men and women who experience pain and confusion due to a true homosexual orientation. We pray that through all the spiritual and pastoral means available they will recognize Christ's and the Church's love for them and our hope that they will come to live in His peace.

To Live in Christ Jesus

National Conference of Catholic Bishops
Washington, D.C.
November 11, 1976

Excerpt

Some persons find themselves through no fault of their own to have a homosexual orientation. Homosexuals, like everyone else, should not suffer from prejudice against their basic human rights. They have a right to respect, friendship and justice. They should have an active role in the Christian community. Homosexual activity, however, as distinguished from homosexual orientation, is morally wrong. Like heterosexual persons, homosexuals are called to give witness to chastity, avoiding, with God's grace, behavior which is wrong for them, just as nonmarital sexual relations are wrong for heterosexuals. Nonetheless, because heterosexuals can usually look forward to marriage, and homosexuals, while their orientation continues, might not, the Christian community should provide them a special degree of pastoral understanding and care.

Statement on Homosexuality

Archbishop John R. Roach
Saint Paul, Minnesota
January, 1978

The homosexual problem is one which is both real and complex. As such it affords no easy solutions. On the one hand, the Catholic community recognizes and affirms the human dignity and worth of homosexuals as persons, and accordingly calls for the protection of their basic human rights. On the other hand, however, it cannot sanction the gay life-style as a morally acceptable alternative to heterosexual marriage.

Both the Christian tradition and our American nation are committed to the inviolable dignity of the human person. Some persons find themselves to be homosexual in orientation through no fault of their own. It is a matter of injustice when, due to prejudice, they must suffer violation of their basic human rights. Like all persons they have a right to human respect, stable friendships, economic security, and social equality. Social isolation, ridicule and economic deprivation of homosexual behaviour is not compatible with basic social justice. Consequently, both religious and civic leaders must seek ways to assure homosexuals every human and civil right which is their due as persons, without, however, neglecting the rights of the larger community.

With regard to the moral question, leadership in the Catholic community has consistently expressed the conviction that homosexual activity, as distinguished from homosexual orientation, is wrong. The Christian tradition holds in high honor the sexual bond between husband and wife, even regarding it as a special expression of God's love for His people. But homosexual behavior falls far short of this sexual and personal ideal. It lacks both the complementarity which exists between masculine and feminine personalities and the possibility of the deepening that can come through sharing the joys and burdens of parenthood and family living.

Like so many things human, sex is ambivalent. It can be either creative or destructive of relationships and persons. Sexual union within the marriage of man and woman is a moral and human good, but outside such marriage it is misplaced and morally unjustifiable. At the same time it must not be forgotten that homosexuality is a complicated question. Homosexuals have like anyone else a deep need for human relationships. And although sexual expression between two members of the same sex cannot be condoned or regarded as of authentic human value, nevertheless, the churches and society must carefully avoid passing judgment on the inner moral state of any individual.

Homosexuality represents a source of a great deal of suffering and loneliness for many good men and women who did not choose to be homosexual, and are trying as best they can to lead moral, constructive lives in their circumstances. Not being able to look to the normal means of support found in marriage, they deserve a special degree of pastoral consideration from their churches, as well as human understanding and compassion from society.

Pastoral Care for the Homosexual

Cardinal Humberto Medeiros
Boston, Massachusetts
June, 1979

My dear brother priests:

I have chosen the Feast of the Sacred Heart as the occasion for this letter to you because it focuses our attention on the love of the priestly Heart of Jesus for all people. He was sent into the world to reconcile all His brothers and sisters with His Father and lead them to salvation. Since, through sacramental ordination, we share in a unique way in His priestly service, this Feast which celebrates His compassionate and healing love has a singular meaning for us, His priests. We believe He has chosen us not only to accept His special love for us, but also to continue His mission of renewing the human family in Him until He comes in glory. This, I think is what St. Paul had in mind when he wrote:

> And for anyone who is in Christ, there is a new creation; the old creation has gone, and now the new one is here. It is all God's work. It was God who reconciled us to Himself through Christ and gave us the work of handing on this reconciliation. In other words, God in Christ was reconciling the world to Himself, not holding men's faults against them, and He has entrusted to us the news that they are reconciled. So we are ambassadors for Christ; it is as though God were appealing through us, and the appeal that we make in Christ's name is: be reconciled to God. For our sake God made the sinless one into sin, so that in Him we might become the goodness of God. As His fellow workers, we beg you once again not to neglect the grace of God that you have received (2 Cor. 5:17-21; 6:1).

Looking with faith at the Heart of Christ pierced for us, we come to realize how vividly God wishes to reveal to us His loving will that all His children be reconciled to Him. Out of infinite love, symbolized by the human heart, the Father sent His only Son into the world so that through the blood shed by Jesus on the cross, God might reconcile all to Himself (cf. 1 Jn. 4:9-10; Eph. 2:11-18). This is a marvelous mystery indeed! And perhaps more marvelous still is the fact that God calls us to join Him in this stupendous work of divine love, as if He "were appealing through us." *God appealing through us!*

Pastoral Concern for Homosexual People

Because as priests we are not merely ambassadors for Christ, but stand in the midst of the people *in the person* of Christ, we are the ministers of His reconciling and healing love and the bearers of the light of His truth. As human beings, we need His healing and light. As priests we bring His healing to the wounded and

His light to those in darkness and confusion. For this reason, I wish to speak with you on an issue of considerable concern, especially in our time. You know of the confusion in doctrine and pastoral practice which has arisen in recent years regarding those of our brothers and sisters who have homosexual tendencies or engage in homosexual behavior.

I have written at length to you on this matter in the past, and there are several official Church documents which have dealt with it. Nevertheless, the confusion seems to persist. Hopefully, these observations of mine will assist you to help dispel the confusion which seems to afflict the minds and hearts of some, perhaps many.

First of all, we know that there is a segment of our human population who experience significant homosexual inclinations, drives and attraction. In fact, many people experience some such feelings temporarily during their adolescence or in situations where they are living in a *homosocial* environment for an extended period of time. For some, the inclinations seem to persist and are stronger than heterosexual feelings and attractions. It is important to note that human drives, feelings and attractions are ultimately rooted in natural impulse. Unless they are deliberately nurtured and strengthened, they are morally neutral.

The cultural environment in which we live, however, seems to offer confusing advice. Film, drama, literature, television and radio sometimes tend to suggest that homosexual behavior is a morally legitimate alternative in sexual expression.

In recent months, some of us have received a letter from an organization called *Dignity*. In this and other documents including books and tapes, the authors make strong recommendations to us regarding our ministry to homosexual people. For instance, sometimes we are counselled to minister to homosexual brothers and sisters in a special group, to allow only certain priests to minister to them, to accept the theory that homosexuality differs from heterosexuality just as being right-handed differs from being left-handed, to accept the contention that the Church has condemned not only homosexual acts but also the homosexual orientation, to provide liturgies, prayer services, even parishes which are exclusively or primarily for those who are homosexual and, as official representatives of the Church, to accept homosexual unions as preferable to promiscuity. At times, it is even suggested that we are guilty of harming those who are homosexual when we adhere to the moral teaching of the Church.

The attitudes reflected in these recommendations do appeal to the pastoral love of the Church, because basically they bespeak a yearning, however hidden, for healing, for reconciliation. This is true both of those who experience these tendencies and those who try to help them. May we not say that whatever the more specific origin of these attitudes and inclinations may be, fundamentally they arise from the "wounded" human person of whom St. Paul speaks so feelingly? (cf. Rom. 7:14-25). The Second Vatican Council addressed itself to this source of confusion within us and in our social life. The Council is a reflection of St. Paul's analysis and a fruit of the Church's experience. Allow me to quote it:

> The truth is that the imbalances under which the modern world labors are linked with that more basic imbalance rooted in the heart of man. For in man himself many elements wrestle with one another. Thus, on the one hand, as a creature he experiences his limitations in a multitude of ways. On the other, he feels himself to be boundless in his desires and summoned to a higher life.
>
> Pulled by manifold attractions, he is constantly forced to choose among them and to renounce some. Indeed as a weak and sinful being, he often does what he would not, and fails to do what he would. Hence he suffers from internal divisions, and from these flow so many and such great discords in society (*Constitution on the Church in the Modern World,* 10).

It appears that confusion and discord come naturally from our "internal divisions," but we seek forever to find new ways to heal this basic wound of our nature. It is not surprising, therefore, that some would press special plans for action on the Church to heal those who experience homosexual pain.

Appreciation of True Dignity in Christ Jesus

The Church listens to the appeal because she is sent to all to heal them, to save them in the power of Christ. That is her mission. On this point we have the eloquent and inspiring words of our Holy Father, Pope John Paul II:

> Jesus Christ is the chief way for the Church. He Himself is our way 'to the Father's house' (cf. Jn. 14:1ff.) and is the way to each man. On this way leading from Christ to man, on this way on which Christ unites Himself with each man, nobody can halt the Church (*The Redeemer of Man,* 13).

He also says:

> The Church cannot abandon man, for his 'destiny,' that is to say his election, calling, birth and death, salvation and perdition, is so closely and unbreakably linked with Christ (*The Redeemer of Man,* 14).

And, finally, Pope John Paul II writes:

> This man is the way for the Church—a way that, in a sense, is the basis for all the other ways that the Church must walk—because man—every man without any exception whatever—has been redeemed by Christ and because with man—with each man without any exception whatever—Christ is in a way united, even when man is unaware of it: 'Christ who died and was raised up for all, provides man'—each and every man—'with the light and the strength to measure up to his supreme calling' (*The Redeemer of Man,* 14).

Precisely who is this man? For the Pope he is not an abstraction. He is a concrete, living human being "in all the truth of his life, in his conscience, in his continual inclinations to sin and at the same time in his continual aspiration to truth, the good, the beautiful, justice and love . . ." (*The Redeemer of Man,* 14). And the Holy Father describes this man or woman for us, lest we think the Church is to deal with man as he might be and not as we find him every day in ourselves and in others. Forgive me the length of this quotation, but it is good for us to keep it in mind in connection with our subject. Pope John Paul II writes:

> We are speaking precisely of each man on this planet, this earth that the Creator gave to the first man, saying to the man and the woman: "Subdue it and have dominion!' (Gn. 1:28). Each man in all the unrepeatable reality of what he is and what he does, of his intellect and will, of his conscience and heart. Man who in his reality has, because he is a 'person,' a history of his life that is his own and, most important, a history of his soul that is his own. Man who, in keeping with the openness of his spirit within and also with the many diverse needs of his body and his existence in time, writes this personal history of his existence in time, writes this personal history of his through numerous bonds, contacts, situations, and social structures linking him with other men, beginning to do so from the first moment of his conception and birth. Man in the full truth of his existence, of his personal being and also of his community and social being—in the sphere of his own family, in the sphere of society and very diverse contexts, in the sphere of his own nation or people (perhaps still only that of his clan or tribe), and in the sphere of the whole of mankind—this man is the primary route that the Church must travel in fulfilling her mission: *He is the primary and fundamental way for the Church,* the way traced out by Christ Himself, the way that leads invariably through the mystery of the Incarnation and the Redemption (*The Redeemer of Man,* 14).

There is no doubt that man and woman as we find them anywhere at any point in history are the center of the pastoral love and concern of the Church. This is every one of us wounded by original sin and our own personal sins and suffering from "internal divisions" which lead to alienation from God, from self and from others. From the basic wound and its consequences Jesus came to heal us. Moreover, we, His priests, have been entrusted with the mission to extend His healing and saving service to every one of our brothers and sisters without exception, no matter what the pain, what the division, what the alienation. Man in his actual condition is the path for the Church and so He is the path for the priests of the Church.

Pastoral Response

There is no question, therefore, that we are called to minister with pastoral love to those of our brothers and sisters who have homosexual inclinations or enter into homosexual behavior. To them as to all others without exception we must bring the riches of the healing love and mercy of the Good Shepherd. We do this in the Church and through the Church to whom the Lord Jesus has entrusted the dispensing of His mysteries and the authentic proclamation of His saving word. Let us listen together to the Second Vatican Council:

> Since the priestly ministry is the ministry of the Church herself, it can be

> discharged only in hierarchical communion with the whole body. Therefore, pastoral love demands that acting in this communion, priests dedicate their own wills through obedience to the service of God and their brothers. This love requires that they accept and carry out in a spirit of faith whatever is commanded or recommended by the Sovereign Pontiff, their own Bishop, or other Superiors (*Decree on the Ministry and Life of Priests,* 15).

We know what the light of Christ through the Church is with regard to our brothers and sisters under consideration. Let us listen to the Holy See:

> At the present time, there are those who, basing themselves on observations in the psychological order, have begun to judge indulgently, and even to excuse completely, homosexual relations between certain people. This they do in opposition to the constant teaching of the Magisterium and to the moral sense of the Christian people.
>
> A distinction is drawn, and it seems with some reason, between homosexuals whose tendency comes from a false education, from a lack of normal sexual development, from habit, from bad example, or from other similar causes, and is transitory or at least not incurable; and homosexuals who are definitely such because of some kind of instinct or a pathological constitution judged to be incurable.
>
> In regard to this second category of subjects, some people conclude that their tendency is so natural that it justifies in their case homosexual relations within a sincere communion of life and love analogous to marriage, insofar as such homosexuals feel incapable of enduring a solitary life.
>
> In the pastoral field, these homosexuals must certainly be treated with understanding and sustained in the hope of overcoming their personal difficulties and their inability to fit into society. Their culpability will be judged with prudence. But no pastoral method can be employed which would give moral justification to these acts on the grounds that they would be consonant with the condition of such people. For according to the objective moral order, homosexual relations are acts which lack an essential and indispensable finality. In Sacred Scripture they are condemned as a serious depravity and even presented as the sad consequence of rejecting God. This judgment of Scripture does not, of course, permit us to conclude that all those who suffer from this anomaly are personally responsible for it, but it does attest to the fact that homosexual acts are intrinsically disordered and can in no case be approved (*Declaration on Sexual Ethics,* 8—Sacred Congregation for the Doctrine of the Faith).

For us as priests to sustain this teaching of the Church and to present it with peace and confidence, we must ourselves accept the Church as bearing in herself the light of Christ. We must also nurture in our own hearts a strong resistance to any self-centered forces in the culture which claim to foster human dignity, but which in fact inhibit and debase it. In the faith of the Church we must see the homosexual person as one whom Christ loves and wants to heal in the light of truth through genuine love.

The homosexual person must be free to seek help from any and all of Christ's priests. On our part, each of us must be ready to respond to such needs. This is a ministry for all of us and we must be prepared to make serious efforts to fulfill it as we do all other aspects of our priestly calling. We do not want to push them aside or cut them off from the mainstream of Catholic and parochial life by encouraging them, even if indirectly, to worship only in a few designated churches or allowing them to be counselled only in a special group or instructing them that they are only to approach one or at most several designated priests for spiritual support. On the human level, such a course on our part would be demeaning. It would deprive them of their rightful place in the whole Church community. And on the spiritual level, this attitude is unchristian. Such segregation would not be sound psychologically, spiritually or pastorally. It is important that we reach out in sacramental ministry to them and give the time and effort of personal counselling and guidance when they need this.

Sometimes such counselling must be done against a background of social pressure that presents the notion so prevalent in our culture today, and even in some theological writings, that homosexual relationships and homosexual acts are not sinful as long as they are "personally enriching." My brother priests, if we accept such a notion, we degrade the person we are counselling—a person for whom Christ shed His blood. Moreover, we destroy the possibility of truly helping the person. You and I must resist this pressure and retain in our hearts the same respect for this individual man or woman that Christ Himself has. Basically, what you and I must desire as we engage in conversation with the individual needing help is that through us he or she can meet Christ. Because of this goal, any acceptance on our part of homosexual acts in themselves or of homosexual life-styles as consonant with Christian living is foreign to our pastoral practice. Such acts and the life-styles which sometimes lead to them debase the human person. They are objectively immoral, even if certain people experience difficulty in moving beyond them. We want to avoid various errors as we try to lead this person to Christ. We must avoid the extreme of the Pharisee; we must resist our own desire for acceptance and popularity on the part of this person or other homosexual people; we must resist the desire to give an easy answer; we must resist the growing thrust toward undiscerning tolerance in our times.

Perhaps we can learn a great deal from an episode in the life of Jesus which is preserved for us in John's gospel (Jn. 8:1-11). When the woman caught in adultery was brought to Jesus, it soon became obvious that the Scribes and Pharisees wanted to trap Jesus with a pastoral dilemma. He had preached mercy toward the sinner; yet the Law was utterly clear in cases where the adultery of a woman could be publicly attested. Jesus refused to be forced to choose between the two proposed alternatives: condone or condemn. "If there is one of you who has not sinned, let him be the first to cast a stone at her" (Jn. 8:7). And they slipped away, one by one. Then that remarkable and touching exchange transpired: "Jesus looked up and said, 'Woman, where are they? Has no one condemned you?' 'No one, sir,' she replied. 'Neither do I condemn you,' said Jesus, 'go away and do not sin any more'" (Jn. 8:10-11). In this simple episode Jesus revealed how God shows mercy without condoning sin. We, His priests, are called to do in like manner.

If we model our approach on Christ Jesus, we will be moved to share in His compassion and understanding, while remaining firm in our adherence to the Church's teaching despite pressures to the contrary. In this connection let us recognize humbly, yet discerningly the significant gift that theologians offer us in the Church. They are called upon to explore new ways of understanding and interpreting God's message for contemporary people. Their probing work is always tentative until tested and refined in and by the Church. In pastoral practice, we must adhere to the theological positions which have been officially incorporated into Church teaching. Thus we are called to do what we can to help the homosexual person lead a chaste life. In doing so, we are accepting a homosexual man or woman as a full member of the Church and of society. When we do this, we are calling the person to that same life of chastity which we try to live. We are calling and helping this person to the same virtue of chastity to which we are encouraging married persons or single members of our flock. We are giving them their full place in the Church. We refuse to relegate them to a "separate but equal" category which ultimately denies them their basic human dignity and Christian nobility.

Experience tells us that in working with homosexual people, we will realize the very great difficulty that many of them—whether married or single—have in avoiding homosexual behavior or in avoiding the places or circumstances which so easily lead to these acts. What will we do? The answer we already know. We will bring them to Christ who alone has the power to strengthen and heal them. We bring them to the person of Christ most directly when they approach us in the Sacrament of Reconciliation. This sacrament is never out of date because Christ always wishes to redeem, to forgive, to release from sin, to heal what is wounded. We bring them to Him in the Holy Eucharist. We bring them to Him by leading them to personal prayer, to the prudent practice of penance and self-denial and to the avoidance of the occasion of sin. We encourage them to sound spiritual reading. We are their friend. We love them—but as Christ loves them—with an intelligent, disciplined and pastoral love.

Some Implications for Our Common Pastoral Practice

I hope that these thoughts are helpful to you. Since this is a pastoral question which touches the whole Archdiocese, I have the responsibility to indicate some specific norms for implementing Church teaching in the local pastoral situation.

(1) All priests are to be open to assisting homosexual people along the lines outlined above. If all of us adopt a stance toward homosexual people which is truly Christ's and the Church's approach, they will be affirmed and drawn to Christ at the same time. If we as priests accept them as Christ accepts them, receive their words with respect, as the words of brothers and sisters, and also observe strict confidentiality as is our duty, we can help them to find their rightful place in the parish without drawing attention to this in a public way. It is this full membership and activity—when coupled with a deep spiritual and sacramental life— which will help them to avoid sin and enable them to grow both spiritually and psychologically. Hence there is no priest specifically assigned to ministry to homosexual people. If there has been any confusion in the past as to what was the actual situation, I trust that this matter is now clear. This is part of the overall ministry of every priest in the Archdiocese of Boston.

(2) We do not want to encourage our people to join so-called "gay groups." Experience also shows that such groups can lead young people who are anxious or confused about their sexual drives to embrace a homosexual culture and even a homosexual way of life. It is possible that the very fact of banding together in such groups for social and religious purposes could include the recognition and even the fostering of homosexual activity. Moreover, I do not authorize any priest in the Archdiocese of Boston to offer the Eucharist for a group who band together as homosexuals. Such groups tend to impede true human and spiritual development. We want to integrate all men and women into the life of our parishes.

(3) We also want to be discerning in this area in recommending candidates for the seminary and ordination. A man who experiences difficulty in handling homosexual drives and feelings will find himself attempting to live a celibate life in an environment which only heightens his struggles. Sometimes such men experience serious liabilities in relating comfortably with women. Or they may find themselves arrested in their emotional development. Only those who have moved beyond genital sexual preoccupation and found a real capacity for marital life and love, can proceed to a celibate life with a reasonable possibility for truly oblative love. I realize that there are varying degrees of homosexuality. Obviously, I am not including the young man who is still struggling to grow and who may experience some homosexual feelings, but gives assurance of moving beyond his tendencies. But it should be our practice to lead an individual person with all his special traits to that state of life where he will find the most peace and be personally best able to live a life of true and unselfish love without having to overcome almost insurmountable obstacles or difficulties.

Conclusion

Pope John Paul II has indicated to us the way we should follow. Let us reflect together on his pastoral guidance, on how to all we must always be priests and shepherds:

It may sometimes seem to us that they do not want this, or that they wish us to be in every way 'like them;' at times it even seems that they demand this of us. And here one very much needs a profound 'sense of faith' and 'the gift of discernment.' In fact, it is very easy to let oneself be guided by appearances and fall victim to a fundamental illusion in what is essential. Those who call for the secularization of priestly life and applaud its manifestations will undoubtedly abandon us when we succumb to temptation. We shall then cease to be necessary and popular. Our time is characterized by different forms of 'manipulation' and 'exploitation' of man, but we cannot give in to any of these. In practical terms, the only priest who will always prove necessary to people is the priest who is conscious of the full meaning of his priesthood; the priest who believes profoundly, who professes his faith with courage, who prays fervently, who teaches with deep conviction, who serves, who puts into practice in his own life the program of the Beatitudes, who knows how to love disinterestedly, who is close to everyone, and especially to those who are in most need.

Our pastoral activity demands that we should be close to people and all their problems, whether these problems be personal, family or social ones, but it also demands that we should be close to all these problems in 'a priestly way.' Only then, in the sphere of all those problems, do we remain ourselves. Therefore, if we are really of assistance in those human problems, and they are sometimes very difficult ones, then we keep our identity and are really faithful to our vocation. With great perspicacity we must seek, together with all men, truth and justice, the true and definitive dimension of which we can only find in the Gospel, or rather in Christ Himself. Our task is to serve truth and justice in the dimensions of human 'temporality,' but always in a perspective that is the perspective of eternal salvation. This salvation takes into account the temporal achievements of the human spirit in the spheres of knowledge and morality, as the Second Vatican Council wonderfully recalled, but it is not identical with them, and in fact it goes higher than them: 'The things that no eye has seen and no ear has heard . . . all that God has prepared for those who love Him.' Our brethren in the faith, and unbelievers too, expect us always to be able to show them this perspective, to become real witnesses to it, to be dispensers of grace, to be servants of the word of God. They expect us to be men of prayer (Letter of John Paul II *To All the Priests of the Church on Holy Thursday,* 1979).

My dear brother priests: this has been a long letter when perhaps a few words of direction might have sufficed. Yet I wished to place this issue, as all other issues affecting the human person and our pastoral love for one another, in the context of the more extended teaching of the Scripture, the Council and our Holy Father. I feel I have not done justice to any of these, but I have tried hard, I prayed and suffered, and I consulted in order to be clear, just and faithful to our mission in Our Lord Jesus Christ. You know that in dealing with the human person, we find each man and each woman to be a mystery hidden with Christ in the God who created us for Himself. Because of this we must appeal to faith to know what to say and what to do in the process of healing any of our brothers and sisters. In the last analysis we must walk in faith. The Council tells us:

> Since all of these realities are hidden with Christ in God they can be best grasped by faith. For the leaders of the People of God must walk by faith, following the example of the faithful Abraham, who in faith 'obeyed by going out into a place which he was to receive for an inheritance; and he went out, not knowing where he was going (Heb. 11:8). The dispenser of the mysteries of God can be truly compared to the man who sowed his field and of whom the Lord said: 'Then he slept and rose, night and day; and the seed sprouted and grew without his knowing it' (Mk. 4:27) (*Decree on the Ministry and Life of Priests,* 22).

And so we walk by faith in the Son of God who loved us and gave Himself up for us (cf.. Gal. 2:20) as we embrace in pastoral love all our bothers and sisters we can reach to bring the healing grace of our Divine Redeemer.

With priestly affection and a hearty blessing, I am

Devotedly yours in Our Lord,
Humberto Cardinal Medeiros
Archbishop of Boston

A Pastoral Letter on Homosexuality

Archbishop John R. Quinn
San Francisco, California

May 5, 1980

To the Priests, Deacons, Religious and all the Faithful of Christ in the Archdiocese of San Francisco: Grace and peace be yours from God our Father and from the Lord, Jesus Christ!

PART I: PRESENT-DAY SITUATION

Vexing and serious questions arise with increasing frequency concerning the problem of homosexuality. While I cannot either treat or answer all possible questions on the subject, I feel it timely and important to offer some guidance and bring, I hope, some clarity to our understanding of the issue. It is with this purpose, then, that I write to you and commend to you the thoughts which follow in this pastoral letter.

A survey of the literature on the subject of homosexuality reveals that since 1974 especially, there has been a growing public affirmation by individuals of their own homosexuality. At the same time pressures have been growing to remove prejudicial attitudes toward homosexual persons especially in regard to housing, hiring practices, teaching opportunities, etc. Still more there are growing pressures calling for recognition of the homosexual lifestyle as legitimate and worthy of societal, legal and ecclesiastical endorsement and approval.

In short, we are being besieged to move from a non-prejudicial attitude toward individuals to a point of view of total acceptance of homosexuality as a legitimate personal and public choice. Thus homosexuality is seen as a legitimate alternative to heterosexuality and the society is asked to support this position. Does this position warrant our agreement?

Several years ago, Jaroslav Pelikan attempted to crystallize the essence of the Catholic Church in the formula: *identity plus universality*. "By identity I mean that which distinguishes the Church from the world—its message, its uniqueness, its particularity. By universality, on the other hand, I mean that which impels the Church to embrace nothing less than all mankind in its vision and its appeal." The general trend we are speaking of in regard to homosexuality reveals a determined bias toward the pole of universality resulting in a distorted under-emphasis on the pole of identity. Here it is well to recall Pope John Paul's reminder that the Church must be a "sign of contradiction" to those elements of the world which threaten to distort, harm or destroy the authentic message of Christ.

And so as we move into the final decades marking two thousand years since the birth of Christ, the Church is keenly aware of a new and transforming consciousness of universality. But for the Church this new consciousness stands within the perspective of a clear, certain and unambiguous Catholic identity which is embodied in the Church's Faith and witness to Jesus Christ. Any effort, then, to deal with the question of homosexuality must have clearly in mind both poles of universality and identity and must be built on the recognition that the Gospel is not a dichotomy between love and truth, for God who is love, is also proclaimed by the Scriptures as Truth, and Jesus said of Himself, "I am the truth."

I. Statement of the Question

There are several reasons why it is not easy to achieve a balanced and objective understanding of homosexuality. First of all, it is a highly charged emotional issue. Thus when certain mitigating factors at the subjective level are correctly pointed out, or when the human rights of homosexual individuals are defended, some wrongly conclude that this means an endorsement of homosexual activity. In addition to the high emotions surrounding the issue, homosexuality in itself is enormously complex in its origins, its psychological vectors, medical ramifications, societal norms and in the application of valid moral principles to individual cases. Hence some of the aspects of the question do not admit of easy answers. This does not at all say that the moral teaching of the Church is unclear. It does say that it is necessary to recognize that we are dealing with an issue of considerable complexity in all dimensions.

Since not all persons who are homosexual engage in homosexual conduct, it is necessary at the outset to make the distinction between homosexual tendency and the acting out of homosexuality through specifically sexual encounters with persons of the same sex. It must also be pointed out that there is often a difference in understanding the language used in discussing homosexuality. For instance, moral theologians tend to use the expression "homosexual orientation" to mean only the psychosexual attraction itself. On the other hand, legislative language often uses the expression "homosexual orientation" not merely for the psychosexual attraction but also to include homosexual acts. For this reason the terminology used here is "homosexual attraction" or "tendency." With this distinction in mind and respecting the contemporary data that in most cases the homosexual tendency has not been chosen, a working definition of homosexuality is: a predominant, persistent, and exclusive psychosexual attraction toward persons of the same sex; a homosexual person is one who feels sexual desire for and a sexual responsiveness to persons of the same sex and who seeks or would like to seek actual sexual fulfillment of this desire by sexual acts with a person of the same sex. This definition rightly emphasizes the distinction between the homosexual condition, attraction or tendency, and homosexual acts.

II. Context for Our Response

The major theme of Pope John Paul's first encyclical, *Redemptor hominis,* is, ". . . again and always man" (no. 16). The whole encyclical is a powerful advocacy of respect and reverence for the dignity of the human person. Affirming that moral and spiritual progress is a necessity, the Pope goes on to raise the question whether "man, as man, is developing and progressing or is he regressing and being degraded in his humanity?" (no. 15). The encyclical thus indicates an awareness of the tensions we have already mentioned between identity and universality. The Holy Father acknowledges the need to understand every person, every system, every legitimate right (universality). But he clearly notes that this does not mean "losing certitude about one's own faith or weakening the principles of morality . . ." (no. 6).

This strong sense of certitude—identity—is seen in the encyclical always in the context of love, a love that is greater than sin and weakness and the futility of creation. "It is stronger than death; it is a love always ready to raise up and forgive, always ready to go to meet the prodigal son, always looking for "the revealing of the sons of God." This revelation of love is also described as mercy; and in man's history this revelation of love and mercy has taken a form and a name: that of Jesus Christ" (no. 9).

The Pope thus calls us to draw near to Christ—with all our unrest, uncertainties, weaknesses and sinfulness. We must learn to "appropriate and assimilate the whole of the reality of the incarnation and redemption" (no. 10) in order to find authentic meaning. Moral identity, in other words, must be rooted in the person of Jesus Christ, and it is to this end that the Church must fully dedicate herself (no. 13). And so the Church must always safeguard and proclaim the true calling and the true dignity of humanity by holding in reverence the "transcendence of the human person" (no. 13) immeasurably enhanced by the incarnation, death and resurrection of the Son of God who became like us in all things but sin so that we might become one with Him.

In responding to any moral question, then, we must keep a correct perspective concerning human dignity and transcendence. Our perspective derives from the Gospel and not from any ideology. The teaching of the Faith and the Lord's supreme commandment of love rooted in truth must always underlie our analysis of this and every other moral question.

Recent Catholic teaching on the subject of homosexuality has approached the subject from the point of charity and the inherent dignity of the human person. In 1974 the Bishops of the United States issued a document entitled *Principles To Guide Confessors in Questions of Homosexuality*. The document clearly reaffirms the objective gravity of homosexual acts. At the same time it counsels sensitivity toward the individual homosexual person. The confessor, steering a course between harshness and permissiveness, should manifest great understanding, should give patient and loving encouragement to the individual in the often tedious and discouraging journey to grow in the image of Christ. Similarly, in 1975 the Sacred Congregation for the Doctrine of the Faith issued a document entitled *Declaration on Certain Questions Concerning Sexual Ethics*. This authentic document of the Holy See also reconfirms the objective wrongness of homosexual acts while drawing the important distinction between homosexual acts and a homosexual tendency or attraction.

Then in 1976 the American Bishops wrote a lengthy pastoral letter touching on a variety of moral issues and bearing the title, *To Live in Christ Jesus*. The teaching mentioned in the previous two documents is again stated. In addition, the pastoral letter adds the counsel that homosexual men and women should not suffer from prejudice on the basis of their sexual attraction. In fact, it states, the Christian community should provide a special degree of pastoral care and understanding for the special problems of the homosexual person.

Most recently the Pope himself spoke about homosexuality to the Bishops of the United States in Chicago on October 4, 1979. He said, "As 'men with the message of truth and the power of God' (2 Cor. 6:7), as authentic teachers of God's law and as compassionate pastors, you also rightly stated 'Homosexual activity . . . as distinguished from homosexual orientation, is morally wrong.' In the clarity of this truth, you exemplified the real charity of Christ; you did not betray those people who, because of homosexuality, are confronted with difficult moral problems, as would have happened if, in the name of understanding and compassion, or for any other reason, you had held out false hope to any brother or sister. Rather by your witness to the truth of humanity in God's plan, you effectively manifested fraternal love, upholding the true dignity, the true human dignity, of those who look to Christ's Church for the guidance which comes from the light of God's word."

The recent teachings of the Church therefore re-echo the clear teaching of the Scriptures in declaring homosexual acts to be gravely evil and a disordered use of the sexual faculty. These same teachings, also, make clear distinction between homosexual acts and homosexual orientation and counsel sensitive and positive pastoral care in helping individual homosexual persons in their journey of discipleship.

The question then arises: What must be said to a subculture which advocates removing any distinction between homosexuality and heterosexuality? Given the fact that the authentic teaching of the Church clearly affirms the objective gravity of homosexual acts, what must be said in light of the growing acceptance of homosexuality as a legitimate and alternate lifestyle?

III. The Real Problem

The term "homosexuality" is frequently used as if its meaning and connotations were self-evident. In fact, such is not the case. We have already noted how the term may apply either to a homosexual attraction or to homosexual conduct. In addition, we note that a fairly common view is that homosexuality represents an acquired condition that is both psychological and pathological. Yet many others do not accept homosexuality as pathological and view it as a variant form of sexual behavior. Some schools of thought hold that homosexuality is a purely physiological condition while others consider it only as a physiological pre-disposition. These complexities in the data indicate the wide diversity of homosexual behaviors and only serve to increase the difficulty of arriving at a simple understanding of the problem. From a psychological point of view, homosexuality both in its origins and in its manifestations, is a highly complex phenomenon and not always clearly understood even by experts.

Yet, it is because of developments in the fields of psychology and sociology that Catholic moral theology, guided by the distinction between sexual attraction and sexual behavior, is able to recognize more clearly factors which may in the case of individual conduct mitigate the gravity of such conduct on the subjective level. But an additional problem arises for moral theology in a climate that increasingly encourages public revelation and proclamation of one's homosexual orientation. The emerging visibility of homosexuals and the militancy of the so-called "gay rights" movement only serve to heighten the problem. Still it is in light of this problem that the Church must continue to uphold the human dignity and the human rights of every person including homosexual persons.

On the one hand, then, homosexuality cannot be treated simply as the manifestation of a consciously chosen depravity. Homosexual persons cannot, merely because they are homosexual, be visited with harassment and contempt. The lynch gang approach cannot be justified.

At the same time, however, opposition to homosexuality as a form of conduct, opposition to homosexuality as an acceptable lifestyle, by the Church or by society, cannot be regarded as a prejudice.

To agree that the persecution and harassment of homosexuals is incompatible with the Gospel is, therefore, not to say that the Church and society should be neutral about homosexual activity. The Church and society cannot and should not place the family which is and always will be the basic unit of society on a par with homosexual social units. While we do not possess complete historical data on the subject, the fact is that in no culture has homosexuality been the dominant form of sexual expression, and in Judaism and Christianity homosexual behavior has been clearly and consistently rejected as gravely contrary to the law of God.

PART II: BIBLICAL DATA

Unfortunately biblical scholars have published very little in recent years on the question of homosexuality in the Bible. As a result, a number of writers not trained in the discipline of biblical studies have attempted to address this question within the larger context of homosexuality as a pastoral problem. Most of these studies, regrettably, have not accurately interpreted the scriptural data and are therefore of little real value.

Before considering some individual scriptural texts it will be helpful to make a few general observations. First, the Bible is not merely a textbook of ethics, any more than it is a textbook of science or sociology. There is, of course, no question that the Bible contains ethical teachings concerning certain actions, but these are usually considered from a definite and well-defined point of view. For example, the Old Testament Israelite was commanded, "Thou shalt not kill." He would understand this as pertaining to the society within which he lived and would thus see no contradiction when he killed foreigners in taking over the Promised Land. Consequently, the biblical writers did not necessarily see or experience all the aspects of a moral issue as we would comprehend it today. In other words, they did not necessarily ask the same questions about a given ethical or moral issue which we would ask today. Hence we cannot expect the Scriptures of themselves to provide immediate answers to all of the moral problems that concern us.

Then, too, we must remember that while the Scriptures hold a unique place in God's revelation to man, they are not self-interpreting. The true and authentic interpretation of the Scriptures cannot be accomplished merely and exclusively by a recourse to exegetical and hermeneutical methodologies, as important as these are. Ultimately the authentic interpretation of the Scriptures lies with the living Magisterium of the church which has received from Christ the authority and the grace to determine the true meaning of the Scriptures for People of God. Hence all examination of the Scriptures must be accompanied by recourse to the divine and living tradition of the Magisterium of the Church to which indeed the Scriptures themselves bear witness.

With this in mind, it will be useful to take up several of the more important Scriptural passages which deal with homosexuality.

I. The Old Testament

1. The Men of Sodom (Gn. 19:1-11; cf. Jgs. 19:16-26)

A number of moral evils are involved in this episode. In both accounts a major sin is the refusal to show hospitality which was a sacred obligation throughout the ancient Near East. But this is not the only sin involved. Despite the contentions of a few, there can be no doubt that the verb "know" in both texts refers to sexual intercourse. Without any doubt the attempted rape serves to augment the evil of the incident. These texts, then, cannot be alleged either to approve of or to ignore the homosexual element of the incidents described.

2. David and Jonathan (1 Sm. 18-20; 2 Sm. 1:26)

In some ways, of course, it is not surprising that a western reader would interpret the close friendship between David and Jonathan as a homosexual relationship. And if this view were correct it would be evidence for a tacit approval of such a relationship by the writers of the Old Testament.

But a closer study of the texts shows that the language used to describe their relationship is unmistakably drawn from the terminology of covenants between nations or individuals, such as the statement that "Jonathan loved him [David] as his own soul" (1 Sm. 18:1, 3). This is covenant terminology. It is not sexual. The "covenantal" nature of their relationship is evident also from 1 Samuel 18:3, "Then Jonathan made a **covenant** with David;" and from 20:8, "Deal loyally with me [David], for you have brought me into a covenant with you—a covenant witnessed by the Lord;" also v. 23, "Behold the Lord is [a witness] between you and me forever."

Nor is their kissing and weeping together any evidence of homosexuality (20:41) since men in the Near East commonly express their friendship more demonstratively than is allowed in our western society.

Finally, there is David's extraordinary tribute to Jonathan: "Your love for me was more wonderful than women's love" (2 Sm. 1:26). Admittedly the language here is very strong, but does not necessarily refer to sexual love. The word for "love" in this passage is used elsewhere not only in a sexual sense but also of God's love for man and man's love for God. And so here we probably have the typical ancient near Eastern praise of men at the expense of women (v.g., cf. Sir. 25:13-25). It also probably reflects David's own personal experience as a king. As a king his marriages were necessarily political and as a result the love element may be assumed to have been considerably less in them than the devotion shown him by his faithful friend, Jonathan.

3. Leviticus 18:12 and 20:13

These are the central Old Testament texts regarding homosexuality. They are found as part of the "Holiness Code" (Lv. 17-26) which is a collection of laws written down or rather edited probably during the Babylonian Exile (587-538 B.C.). All authorities acknowledge, however, that the basic content of these laws is considerably older. The two passages that deal with homosexuality are "You shall not lie with a male as with a woman; it is an abomination" (18:22) and "If a man lies with a male as with a woman, both of them have committed an abomination . . ." (20:13).

There is a widespread popular misconception that these texts prohibit homosexual activity because it is associated with pagan worship. Thus it would not be the **homosexual** aspect of the actions that is condemned, but rather the association with paganism. This view is definitely incorrect. First of all, verses in chapters 18 and 20 which warn against imitating the practices of pagan neighbors date only from the time of the exile. The laws themselves are considerably older. Hence later concerns cannot be read back into the laws themselves. Secondly, Israel was not afraid of borrowing or imitating ideas in neighboring pagan cults.

For instance, the Psalms are largely patterned on Canaanite religious poetry. Solomon's temple was built by Phoenician (i.e., Canaanite) architects and shows a number of striking influences of pagan cults. Some have tried to see in the term "abomination," which occurs in these two passages, a specific reference to idolatrous practice. But the use of the term in the Old Testament is too broad to allow this narrow interpretation (v.g., cf. Prv. 11:1, 20; 12:22, etc.).

Finally, certain authors argue that these laws in Leviticus are of little or no relevance to the Christian today, being chiefly cultic and dietary in nature. It is, of course, true that most of the regulations here do concern such matters. But it is equally true that Leviticus contains ethical material as well. Note, for instance, that the "second great commandment," "Thou shalt love thy neighbor as thyself" is found between the two laws discussed here (19:18). One could hardly deny the "relevance" of this statement for the Christian.

II. The New Testament

The major New Testament statements on homosexuality come either from Paul or the "deutero-Pauline" letters (e.g., 1 Tm.). Before discussing specific texts we should say a word about Paul's attitude toward the Law of the Old Testament. Some writers on the issue of homosexuality contend that Paul abrogated the Law by which they mean that the Old Testament ethical requirements were no longer in force. This is a fatuous and dangerously misleading position. Paul's point was that one who is baptized into Christ no longer acts from external motivation (the Law) but from the inner guidance of the Holy Spirit. Yet the *results* of such a teaching—i.e., how a person actually *lived*—would be what any Jew would recognize as a "moral" life, even from the Old Testament viewpoint. Thus the list of qualities Paul regards as essential to "walking in the Spirit" and their opposites (Gal. 5:16-24) is similar to lists of virtues and vices from both contemporary Jewish and pagan sources. Paul does not hesitate to condemn forcefully what is clearly called immoral behavior (v.g., 1 Cor. 5:1-5).

1. Romans 1:18-32

In this passage we are dealing with two things. First, the cause of homosexuality in pagan society and, secondly, the moral judgment on homosexuality. In this passage, then, Paul reflects a common Jewish notion of his time, namely, that certain vices particularly abhorrent to Jews were the result of or a punishment for idolatry. One of these vices is homosexual intercourse. Note that Paul presents this as a perversion of the natural order of things. Of this there can be no doubt, since his whole point is that such "perversity" is the fitting punishment from God for those who refuse to worship Him as true God but pervert the order of nature by worshiping created things. Paul's condemnation of homosexual intercourse is clear in this passage. Yet the notion that this activity springs from idolatry is not entirely relevant to the situation today.

2. *1 Corinthians 6:9*

Paul makes it abundantly clear to his Corinthian readers that freedom from the Law does not mean license to practice immorality. His language is quite clear and quite strong. Two groups he lists here among others who will not "inherit the kingdom of God" and these are "catamites" and "sodomites" (vs. 9). The first word denotes the passive partner in an act of homosexual intercourse. The second (cf. also 1 Tm. 1:10), literally means "those who lie (sexually) with males. The claim that this was not one of the standard terms for homosexuals in the ancient world and that hence it would not have been understood by Paul's readers is completely groundless. The meaning of the word is self-evident in Greek.

Here too the popular misconception turns up that Paul's condemnation of homosexual activity simply represents a reaction to certain pagan rites current in Corinth. To maintain this view one would have to believe that Paul, an educated, pious Jew with rabbinical training, had never heard of the prohibition against homosexual intercourse in Leviticus, and that his repudiation of these practices was merely an *ad hoc* response to goings-on in Corinth. The absurdity of such a view is obvious. One should further note that the word Paul uses for "sodomite" in 1 Corinthians 6:9 closely reflects the terminology of Leviticus 20:13—more evidence that his view on homosexuality comes from Old Testament background completed and expanded by the revelation made in Christ Jesus.

Conclusions from Scripture

From the foregoing it is clear that the Scriptures, both the Old and the New Testament, reject and condemn homosexual acts. The Scriptures, it is true, do not explicitly deal with the question of homosexual attraction or with the issue of a homosexual lifestyle. Nevertheless they do most clearly condemn an important element of that lifestyle, namely homosexual intercourse. Hence it is beyond dispute that there is a clear basis in Scripture for the consistent rejection of a homosexual lifestyle as it exists in the moral teaching of the Church including the most recent Church teaching on the subject.

Cultural Notions

While it is clear that the Scriptures condemn homosexual behavior, this does not imply any justification for exploitation of the homosexual or any injury to his or her dignity as a human person. Thus there is a clear difference between the acceptance of homosexual persons as worthy of respect and as having human rights, and approval of the homosexual lifestyle. To make judgments from a Christian and cultural point of view about homosexual behavior is necessary since the Church cannot be expected to deny its moral teaching and simply bless what is a contemporary cultural phenomenon.

The Church certainly does not condemn those who discover within themselves a homosexual attraction or inclination, and it must work to foster better care and guidance for those men and women whom society has often ostracized. The Church must continue to work toward better education about homosexuality. It must tirelessly try to help homosexual men and women accept and live up to the moral teaching which the Church has received from Christ. But in no case can such acceptance or recognition of the homosexual person imply recognition of homosexual behavior as an accepted lifestyle. The claim that homosexuality is simply a variant of normal sexual behavior and exists alongside heterosexuality as an equivalent expression of adult sexual maturation must be rejected. A normalization of homosexuality could only too easily foster and make more public homosexual behavior with the result of eroding the meaning of the family.

Both from the religious point of view as well as for the good of society itself, marriage and the family are realities that must be protected and strengthened. The family not only continues the human race but it also glues it together. The family is the basic and living example of social cohesion. Thus the Second Vatican Council affirmed, "All . . . who exercise influence over communities and social groups should work efficiently for the welfare of marriage and the family. Public authority should regard it as a sacred duty to recognize, protect and promote their authentic nature, to defend public morality and to foster the progress of home life."

PART III: MORAL AND ETHICAL CONSIDERATIONS

The moral teaching of the Church, based on the Scriptures themselves and consistent in all periods of history, holds that homosexual behavior is objectively immoral, a human disvalue, disordered. The teaching of the Church recognized the fact that homosexuality has generally not been chosen by a person but rather that most homosexual persons gradually come to the realization that they are homosexual. Thus the Church proposes various guidelines and pastoral approaches to assist and encourage the homosexual person's psychological and spiritual growth (cf., v.g., *Principles To Guide Confessors in Questions of Homosexuality*, 1974).

The Church recognizes the complexity of the question as it exists in the life of an individual person as well as the complexity of the question in the fields of the behavioral sciences. There must be sensitivity in treating the question. Homosexual persons must be helped and encouraged to strive for wholeness and personal integrity as indeed all other persons must be encouraged, homosexual or heterosexual. Sexual intercourse cannot be legitimated merely by individual preference or on the basis of sociological surveys or because of mutual consent between two parties. Sexual intercourse is legitimate and morally good only between husband and wife. Thus while it is claimed that homosexuality in a few instances is more or less fulfilling for a limited number of individuals, the homosexual condition and homosexual behavior cannot be morally nominative.

The Church always remains the Church of the Eucharist and of the Sacrament of Penance. Every member of the Church should pray daily, and many times daily, the prayer the Lord has taught us, "Forgive us our trespasses as we forgive those who trespass against us." While the Eucharist does manifest the community aspects of the Church, it cannot be treated merely as an 'occasion' for manifesting this brotherhood" (*Redemptor hominis,* no. 20). More is required.

And so in this connection we must focus attention on the most recent Encyclical Letter of Pope John Paul II on the holy Eucharist. He states, "We cannot allow the life of our communities to lose the good quality of sensitivity of conscience. A sensitive conscience is guided solely by respect for Christ who, when He is received in the Eucharist, should find in the heart of each of us a worthy abode. This question is linked not only with the practice of the Sacrament of Penance but also with a correct sense of responsibility for the whole deposit of moral teaching and for the precise distinction between good and evil . . ." (no. 11).

In order to receive the Eucharist, one must be in the state of grace, that is, in a living union with Christ characterized by the absence of grave sin. One must also be living in harmony with the moral and doctrinal teaching of the Church.

Consequently, just as unmarried persons are not exempt from the moral teaching of the Scriptures and of the Church which has to do with sexual conduct, so homosexual persons are not exempt from this teaching either. Thus despite the difficulties, homosexual persons who wish to receive the Eucharist must be honestly following the moral teaching of the Church or at least sincerely striving to live up to that teaching. This implies that like other Christians they must take advantage of the powerful graces that come from the reverent and frequent recourse to the Sacrament of Penance. In addition, of course, the natural aids they may need such as counseling, psychological help, etc., should and must be used where indicated and as needed. In any case there is nothing to justify a departure from the Church's normative pastoral and doctrinal teaching that one who has sinned gravely cannot approach the Eucharist until he has been absolved from that sin in the Sacrament of Penance and this of course implies the firm amendment on the part of the penitent and his conscious intention to avoid that sin in the future.

Conclusion

Homosexual behavior cannot be viewed as an acceptable form of behavior morally or socially. At the same time persons who are homosexual must be treated with respect as human persons and they have a right to sound pastoral care.

It is the place of the Church and her ministers to speak the whole moral teaching of the Gospel with clarity. The members of the Church have the right to this even when the moral teaching is difficult. But the ministers of the Church must present that moral teaching in a way that also encourages homosexual men and women to begin or to continue the journey toward the fulfillment of the law of Christ.

On the other hand, when homosexual men and women claim that their way of life is a morally healthy one, insist on their intention to affirm and promote it publicly and ask that it be in some way approved by the Church, they are clearly in contempt of the Christian conscience and in conflict with the teaching of the Scriptures.

Indeed the Church holds that there is no place for discrimination and prejudice against a person because of sexual attraction. But this does not mean that there is nothing wrong with homosexual conduct.

While homosexuality may constitute a unique problem and challenge for the homosexual man and woman, it is a mistake to isolate the homosexual person from the general body of disciples. All believers in Christ, young and old, men and women, experience the weight of sin in their lives. All must experience the struggle with evil. All must hear the voice of Christ enjoining His followers to enter on "the narrow way that leads to life," to "take up the cross each day and follow me." Christ chose the way of the cross. There is no other way for His followers. This is true of the homosexual as it is of all other Christians.

But in the Eucharist and in the Sacrament of Penance, supported by a life of daily prayer and growing faith, every believer finds that what is judged impossible by the world is indeed possible. For as Jesus said, "All things are possible to him who believes."

Take to heart, then, the word of God which tells us, "Get rid of all bitterness, all passion and anger, harsh words, slander, and malice of every kind. In place of these, be kind to one another, compassionate, and mutually forgiving, just as God has forgiven you in Christ . . . There was a time when you were in darkness, but now you are light in the Lord. Well, then, live as children of light. Light produces every kind of goodness and justice and truth" (Eph. 4:31-5:9).

Your Servant in Christ Jesus,
+ John R. Quinn
Archbishop of San Francisco

May 5, 1980

Who Is Our Neighbor?

Archbishop Rembert Weakland
Milwaukee, Wisconsin

July 19, 1980

One of the most important tasks facing us in the Church today is addressing the Gospel to various groups of people who have left the Church or who have been left out of — or denied access to — life in the Christian community. Unfortunately, as so often happens, these groups have to band together in a show of force to demand recognition. Two groups, of different nature but still needing our attention, are the divorced and Gay people. In this article I will deal only with the latter.

First, I would like to state that I do not have all the answers in this highly complex issue, but it seems to me that we should begin by approaching it with a sense of calm and prayerful searching, remembering the compassion Jesus had for people who were struggling to find the Kingdom. He saw through the labels that society pinned on Gentiles, tax-collectors, and prostitutes and recognized beneath these name-tags persons worth caring about, simply because they, too, were sons and daughters of His heavenly Father.

Second, it is important for us to know that the Bishops of the United States in a pastoral letter in 1976 called ''To Live in Christ Jesus'' officially stated that homosexuality as a condition is not sinful. This realization can be of immense help to the homosexual who thus knows that deep down there is nothing to separate him or her from God's love and care.

It is true that both in the Old and New Testament the condemnation of acts of homosexuality is strong. Current biblical scholarship has been of tremendous help in bringing these and similar texts into a total cultural context. Homosexuality in the Old Testament was also a ''national security problem'' for a people constantly faced with a need for a male population sufficient to defend itself.

Jesus says nothing specific about homosexuality. But Saint Paul is quite explicit: he is indeed harsh with heterosexuals engaging in homosexual activity; he spoke out strongly against homosexual activity during his missionary journeys to those areas where such activity was associated with orgiastic pagan ritual sacrifices — as it had been, also, in Old Testament times.

All these texts do exist and cannot be taken lightly, even if our knowledge of psychology and the make-up of the human person is vastly different today from Saint Paul's.

Theorists are divided as to the causes of a same-sex orientation. Whether it is biological or environmental, we must accept the fact that many have sincerely tried to be ''healed'' of their ''sickness.''

Experience shows that very few, even with the best therapists, are capable of changing their sexual orientation. Many are coming to the realization that God loves them as they are and that He invites them to open out in concern for others. This movement of grace cannot be ignored or discounted. Many are seeking the opportunity to grow.

Current Church teaching which we Catholics must adhere to expects Gay people to remain celibate, a position which is difficult for them to accept, but, frankly, one which I cannot sidestep. Pope John Paul II, in his talk to the American Bishops in Chicago, after quoting the Bishops' statement that "homosexual activity . . . as distinguished from homosexual orientation, is morally wrong," then warns about holding out false hopes when confronted with such difficult moral problems. I do not take his warning to mean that such situations should not be realistically confronted nor that all hope and pastoral care are to be abandoned.

I look for more dialogue among the grass roots level, our pastoral ministers, and academic people in all fields, so that all sides can contribute to a deeper understanding of this complex moral issue.

Thirdly, the Bishops stated in that same pastoral letter: "Homosexuals, like everyone else, should not suffer from prejudice against their basic human rights. They have a right to respect, friendship, and justice. They should have an active role in the Christian community."

We have to see Gay people then, not as an enemy to be battered down, but as persons worthy of respect and friendship. Many are sincerely seeking to experience the presence of God in their lives and long to be accepted as having something to offer to the building up of the community of believers. They too believe in — Jesus — but that does not alter their sexual orientation.

In justice, I would hope that we can grow beyond the myths surrounding the Gay person, myths, for example, that picture all Gays as perverters of children — a picture that simply is not true.

We must be concerned, also, about their rights. Consequently, I cannot believe it is a Christian attitude that would block them from holding responsible positions in the community.

It seems clear to me that Gay people — like all of us — fare better when they are able to develop stable relationships, when they are not relegated to a same-sex society, when they are permitted to contribute their talents to relieving injustices in our society, when they are loved and respected as people striving to grow, humanly and spiritually.

I invite all in the Catholic community to join me in showing this kind of respect as we try to work out the rightful place of these people in Church life. I ask for calm, careful study, prayer, and reflection so that we can assist all members of society in the exercise of their rights, so that no one is treated as a second-class citizen or as somehow "contaminated."

Come write in the sand with me. Who is going to throw the first stone?

A Ministry to Lesbian and Gay Catholic Persons

The Roman Catholic Church of Baltimore
Baltimore, Maryland

October 5, 1981

The spirit of the Lord has been given to me,
for he has anointed me.
He has sent me to bring the good news to the poor,
to proclaim liberty to captives
and to the blind new sight,
to set the downtrodden free,
to proclaim the Lord's year of favor.
—The Gospel of St. Luke, 4:18

With these words, Christ declared and described His mission in the world. He came to bring salvation: a salvation that was to transform the heart of the individual and to remake the face of the earth as well. At the center of this salvation, at the core of the Reign of God He announced was a concern for and a promise of justice. In the words of Pope John Paul II: " The redemption of the world—this tremendous mystery of love in which creation is renewed—is, at its deepest root, the fullness of justice in a human heart—the heart of the first-born Son—in order that it may become justice in the hearts of many human beings, predestined from eternity in the first-born Son to be children of God and called to grace, called to love."

In carrying out His mission, Christ reached out in a special way to the poor—to the widow and the orphan, to the powerless and the despised. But, in so doing, He never separated himself from them; He was one with them; He made their cause his own. He thereby revealed not only His special concern for the poor but the special place they hold in the drama of salvation.

The Church, being faithful to Christ, continues His mission in its ministry; through word and deed, the Church proclaims the presence of God's reign among us; directed and empowered by the Spirit, it labors for the full realization of that reign. Toward that end, it not only reaches out to help the poor, the powerless, the despised; but as Christ did, it takes their part and makes their cause its own.

While this ministry is at the core of all the Church is about, the Church finds it necessary at times to formalize and make public its ministry to certain groups within society. Whenever a particular group of people are denied their basic human rights and suffer violence to their human dignity because of prejudice or misunderstanding, there is injustice. In the face of that injustice, the Church cannot remain silent and still be true to its mission. Thus, the Church has established a special ministry to the black and the Hispanic communities, to the handicapped and the elderly.

Such is the situation of people in our society known as "homosexual".

The term "homosexual" admits of different meanings. Sometimes it is used to identify an individual with a predominant and persistent psychosexual attraction toward persons of the same gender. At other times "homosexual" is used to describe specific forms of behavior occurring between persons of the same gender. In the former instance, the term refers to something more than particular types of actions; it signifies the general orientation and tenor of one's total self by which one is drawn in many ways and at many different levels to persons of the same rather than the opposite gender. (On the basis of this differentiation between homosexual orientation and homosexual behavior, it is possible—and indeed happens—that homosexual behavior may occur between people with a heterosexual orientation as well as between people with homosexual orientation.) Throughout this statement, the term "homosexual" will be used to refer to persons with a predominant and persistent psychosexual attraction toward others of the same gender.

Because of prejudice and misunderstanding, men and women with a homosexual orientation (more properly spoken of as gays and lesbians) have suffered public ridicule, social exclusion and economic hardship, thereby denigrating their human dignity by denying them respect, equality and full participation in society. Therefore, the Roman Catholic Church of Baltimore is setting up a formal and public ministry to gay and lesbian people to bear witness to its opposition to the injustice they have suffered and are suffering.

At the same time, we are mindful of the warning and challenge issued by Pope Paul VI: "It is too easy to throw back on others responsibility for injustice, if at the same time one does not realize how each one shares in it personally, and how personal conversion is needed first." In the past, we Roman Catholics have been called upon to recognize in our lives the presence of such injustices as racism and blindness to the poor, and to be converted. Thus, even as we focus attention on the injustices suffered by gays and lesbians because of the prejudices and misunderstandings of society, we cannot overlook injustices they have encountered within our own Church—injustices such as denial of respect and of full participation in the community. Therefore, in formalizing and making public this ministry to gay and lesbian people, we Roman Catholics must also examine our own hearts and recognize where we personally stand in need of conversion because of our own participation in these injustices.

This formal, public ministry to gay and lesbian people is being established as well because many gays and lesbians who are Roman Catholics have expressed the feeling that they are misunderstoood by the Church, even that they are being deserted by the Church. The Roman Catholic Church of Baltimore wants to make it clear to all that we have not forgotten these people. We are concerned to respond to their needs—needs which are exacerbated by the injustices which they suffer.

In establishing this formal, public ministry, we not only call upon society to overcome its injustice, we address a message to gays and lesbians as well. We repeat, as the Church has done in every age, the challenge Christ has laid before people: "Be perfect as your heavenly Father is perfect." Not only must we demand from others respect for our dignity as human beings, we must live in such a way as to respect our own dignity. We must do justice to our personhood, for we have been created in the image and likeness of God.

Our response to Christ's call to perfection must be total, that is, it must be made at every level of who we are as persons. Heart and mind, body and spirit—all have to be developed and integrated to the fullest of our abilities; that alone is fitting gratitude for the great gifts God has bestowed on us. But, as Christ's command of love so clearly shows, we develop and integrate ourselves only as we reach out to others. Thus, we are to bring friendship and healing into the lives of other individuals; and we are to work toward the betterment of our culture and society so that all people may live together as brothers and sisters in a world marked by justice and peace.

With regard to our sexuality, this call to perfection is a call to form our lives according to the virtue of chastity. Far from being a denial of our sexuality, this virtue is grounded in our belief that sexuality is a gift from God, a creation that God saw as "very good." Through chastity, we strive to live out our sexuality to the full of its human potential. This virtue increases the human person's dignity and enables one to love truly, disinterestedly, unselfishly and with respect for others," (as the Sacred Congregation for the Doctrine of the Faith explained). This call to perfection through a life of chastity is addressed to all people, whether their orientation be heterosexual or homosexual, single or married.

The demands this virtue makes on us individuals depends on our particular state of life. Every expression of our sexuality, whether it be a word, an embrace, a kiss or the marital act of intercourse, falls under the demand of love. For, sexuality "as an aspect of personality which lets us enter other persons' lives as friends and encourages them to enter our lives...is a relational power which includes the qualities of sensitivity, understanding, warmth, openness to persons, compassion and mutual support," (the Most Rev. Francis J. Mugavero wrote). Any expression of our sexuality that is not informed by these qualities demeans not only another person, but our own person as well. The genital expression of our sexuality achieves its unique and fullest meaning within a context of life-giving and commitment. These obligations connected with sexual expression, arising as they do from the very meaning of human sexuality, bind all people, whether their orientation be heterosexual or homosexual.

Accordingly, the homosexual orientation is in no way held to be a sinful condition. Like heterosexuality, it represents the situation in which one finds oneself, and so the starting point for one's response to Christ's call to perfection. Responding to this call does not mean that one must change this orientation. Rather, it entails living out the demands of chastity within that orientation.

In setting before gays and lesbians Christ's call to perfection, the Church also reminds them that they are to respond personally to this call, that central to this response is conscience; i.e., a properly formed conscience. Such a response involves more than merely the learning or internalization of moral rules. Proper formation of conscience requires that an individual make an integral part of himself or herself the "Christian principles inherent in the truths that Christ revealed," (Archbishop Borders wrote). As such, they are part of who one is and what one stands for when an individual confronts a concrete situation within which a moral decision must be made. In making such a decision, "the role of the conscience is that of a judge, not a teacher;... conscience does not teach what is good or evil, nor does it create good or evil. It weighs accumulated data, makes a judgement in very concrete, not theoretical, situations, the concrete situations;" of one's life, (Archbishop Borders continued).

The ministry of the Roman Catholic Church to gays and lesbians which finds expression in the call to perfection and in the challenge to respond out of a properly formed conscience is always a pastoral ministry. It is a ministry which is not content merely to repeat the challenge Christ sets before each generation; it seeks to work with each individual, taking into account that person's particular strengths and weaknesses, and helping that person make the fullest response possible at this moment in his or her life. This pastoral concern for the individual has sometimes given people the impression that the Church no longer takes a stand on the meaning and demands of sexuality and that it allows the individual to do whatever he or she wants. Such is not the case, as the tenor of this document clearly shows. The only way the Church could make certain that such an impression would not be taken would be for the Church to stop using a pastoral approach to ministry. Should that be done, however, Christ's call to perfection could appear as a harsh, impersonal law that is blind to the weaknesses and limitations of the human condition; and the face of a merciful God, as revealed to us so powerfully through Christ, would be covered and lost to sight. The path marked out for the confessor (a priest hearing confession) in the following quotation should be followed by all who minister to gays and lesbians. "The confessor, steering a course between harshness and permissiveness, should manifest great understanding, should give patient and loving encouragement to the individual in the often tedious and discouraging journey to grow in the image of Christ."

To assist in carrying out this pastoral ministry to gays and lesbians, we draw attention to certain areas of concern without in any way trying to be exhaustive. First of all, gays and lesbians must be treated in a way that communicates a respect for and a valuing of them as persons. This, of course, is only what is due them as human beings. But the prejudices and misunderstandings under which they suffer have denied them this. Without a sense of self-worth, of their dignity as human beings, their ability to respond to Christ's call is severely qualified.

Secondly, this respect requires that the identity of a person not be limited to his or her sexual orientation. In the words of (Alan Bell, an author):"...our data appear to indicate that homosexuality involves a large number of widely divergent experiences—developmental, sexual, social and psychological—and that even after a person has been labeled 'homosexual' . . . there is little that can be predicted about the person on the basis of that label."

Thirdly, we must not overlook the detrimental effects that prejudice, misunderstanding, and social exclusion can have on individuals. "Being subject to misunderstanding and at times unjust discrimination has resulted in an overreaction on the part of some persons of homosexual orientation," (Bishop Mugavero wrote). It may also limit the level of response that can be expected from an individual.

Fourthly, a pastoral ministry approach to gays and lesbians, as to all people, is carried out in the spirit of understanding and forgiveness that was Christ's. Here we do well to recall the words of the Roman Catholic bishops of the United States in discussing the issue of artificial contraception. While the context is different, the substance of the message is most appropos. Those who do not fully live up to Christ's call to perfection are urged "...never to lose heart but to continue to take full advantage of the strength which comes from the Sacrament of Penance and the grace, healing, and peace in the Eucharist. May we all be mindful of the invitation of Jesus: 'The one who comes to me I will never turn away'-John 6:37. Humility, awareness of our pilgrim state, a willingness and determination to grow in the likeness of the Risen Christ will help to restore direction of purpose and spiritual stability."

A further reason for establishing a formal public ministry to gays and lesbians is to provide outreach to families. There is a need for structures to which the families of gays and lesbians can turn for support and counsel, and which the families of children struggling with their sexual identity can contact for information and guidance.

A final reason for establishing a formal, public ministry to gay and lesbian people is to set up regular lines of communication by which gays and lesbians can make their voice heard by the Church at large. This is most important for two reasons.

First of all, if ministry to any group is to be successful, it must respond to their real needs. The needs of gays and lesbians cannot be stated for them by those who are not part of that group; for, as past history has shown, such an approach too often results in our responding on the basis of an artificial, even distorted picture. Gays and lesbians must have the freedom as well as the means to make known to the whole Church the needs they have.

Secondly, the Church must listen to gays and lesbians to learn what they have to teach about the saving presence of Christ among us. As the scriptures show over and over again, God takes the side of the poor and the oppressed. But more is involved than that. Jeremiah the prophet brings this out well when he excoriates one of the kings of Israel for not doing as his father before him: "He used to examine the cases of the poor and the needy, then all went well. Is not that what it means to know me?—it is Yahweh who speaks." God not only takes the side of the poor and the oppressed, he makes Himself known through them. Thus, as a people who hunger for the Word of God, we must open our ears to His every message.

These, then, are the reasons why it is both appropriate and essential that a formal, public ministry to gays and lesbians be established in the Roman Catholic Church of Baltimore. We Roman Catholics must set ourselves against the injustice gays and lesbians suffer because of the prejudice and misunderstanding existing both in society and in the Church itself. Gays and lesbians have to hear the call to perfection Christ has given all people as well as the invitation He extends to respond out of a properly formed conscience. There is need for a ministry that is pastoral in nature, taking into account the special needs that gays and lesbians have. There is need for a structure to which families can turn for information and support. Finally, there is need to establish a means of communication by which the Church as a whole can be addressed by gays and lesbians.

Introduction to A Challenge to Love: Gay and Lesbian Catholics in the Church

Bishop Walter Sullivan
Richmond, Virginia

April 28, 1983

Few topics in society today arouse strong, personal feelings in the way occasioned by the subject of this book. Few other issues being discussed in the Catholic community are as difficult and complex from every conceivable angle as the subject of this collection of essays.

Because of the problems surrounding the issue of homosexuality in our society and Church, there is a continuing interest in data from the empirical and social sciences, and an increasing need for balanced and sensitive pastoral responses from all religious denominations. Voices of homosexual Catholics and other Christians are being raised, sometimes in anger and protest, but most often with difficult but sincere questions and genuine, personal concerns about their stance before God, their place in the Church, and the quality of their relationships with others.

In 1976, the American Catholic bishops in their pastoral letter, *To Live in Christ Jesus,* articulated a concise, yet comprehensive and balanced view of homosexuality from a Catholic perspective when they wrote:

> Some persons find themselves, through no fault of their own, to have a homosexual orientation. Homosexuals, like everyone else, should not suffer from prejudice against their basic human rights. They have a right to respect, friendship and justice. They should have an active role in the Christian community. Homosexual activity, however, as distinguished from homosexual orientation, is morally wrong. Like heterosexual persons, homosexuals are called to give witness to chastity, avoiding, with God's grace, behavior which is wrong for them, just as non-marital sexual relations are wrong for heterosexuals. Nonetheless, because heterosexuals can usually look forward to marriage, and homosexuals, while their orientation continues, might not, the Christian community should provide them a special degree of pastoral understanding and care.

Since then, several individual bishops have issued pastoral statements on the topic of homosexuality, or have instituted official forms of ministry to "sexual minorities." In 1975, the *Declaration on Certain Questions Concerning Sexual Ethics* from the Sacred Congregation for the Doctrine of the Faith addressed the topic of homosexuality, and Pope John Paul II, during his visit to the United

States, reaffirmed Church teaching and called upon the bishops to be "compassionate pastors." Several other national hierarchies have issued discussion documents and pastoral guidelines on homosexuality as well. These statements help us to understand the mind of the Church, which has to be taken seriously in any Catholic discussion on homosexuality. Central to this teaching is the fundamental distinction between homosexual *orientation* and homosexual *behavior*.

Yet, we cannot remain satisfied that, once we have clearly articulated the official Church position on homosexuality, nothing else remains to be done in the area of pastoral care for homosexual people and education on this topic for the larger human community, including the families and friends of homosexual people. This is especially true in those cases where the teaching of the Church itself has been presented in such a way that it has been the source or occasion of some of the pain and alienation that many homosexual Catholics experience. We cannot overlook those injustices, including rejection, hostility, or indifference on the part of Christians, that have resulted in a denial of respect or of full participation in the community for homosexual people. We must examine our own hearts and consciences and know that each of us stands in need of real conversion in this area.

While reaffirming its sincere conviction from revelation, tradition, and Christian experience on the meaning of human sexuality, the Church must also provide spiritual and pastoral assistance to those individuals who struggle to integrate a homosexual orientation into a Christian life of deep inner peace. In an age where the flagrant violation of the most basic forms of human rights is so common, we must be especially aware of the need to defend the rights and dignity of every human being, including homosexual people, because of our fundamental belief that each individual, regardless of sexual orientation, is precious in the sight of the Lord and must be no less in ours.

In his pastoral letter, *Who is My Neighbor?,* Rembert Weakland, O.S.B., archbishop of Milwaukee, urges all of us to engage in "more dialogue among the grassroot levels, our pastoral ministers and academic people in all fields so that all sides can contribute to a deeper understanding of this complex moral issue." It is my hope that *A Challenge to Love* will promote that kind of fruitful and life-giving dialogue of which Archbishop Weakland speaks.

Many voices from a wide variety of backgrounds, experiences, and values have been brought together in this effort. All of them come from the Catholic Christian tradition, although not all of them reach the same conclusion. It is vital that we try to listen to them as they attempt to speak to some central issues and to share with us their personal insights on the topic of homosexuality. It is not necessary that we agree with each of them completely, but it is important that we appreciate and respond to their openness, honesty, and courage in writing on this sensitive and often controversial subject from their respective academic disciplines and life experiences. This, in turn, will contribute to that ongoing dialogue that I believe to be so important in the life of the Church today not only on this issue but on so many others that we face as a community of followers of Jesus still on the road of life and truth.

Dialogue by its very nature implies a variety of views and positions: it means degrees of differences and mutual agreement; it may even involve some tension among the participants and at times an inability to reach complete agreement or resolution. Hopefully, mutual sharing will eventually determine whether the differences are real or apparent and whether minor differences can be put aside so that the real issues can be engaged and resolved. Healthy dialogue will ultimately uncover views that are not coherent and arguments that are not sound.

In his encyclical letter *Ecclesiam Suam,* Pope Paul VI wrote at some length about the specific characteristic of dialogue.

> It is an outpouring of thought; it is an invitation to the exercise of the highest powers . . . This very claim would be enough to classify the dialogue among the best manifestations of human activity and culture . . . A second characteristic of the dialogue is meekness . . . The dialogue is not proud; it is not bitter; it is not offensive. Its authority is intrinsic to the truth it explains, to the charity it communicates, to the example it proposes. It is not a command; it is not an imposition; it is peaceful; it avoids violent methods; it is patient; it is generous . . . In the dialogue, one discovers how different are the ways which lead to the light of faith, and how it is possible to make them converge on the same goal. Even if these ways are divergent, they can become complementary by forcing our reasoning process out of the worn paths and by obliging it to deepen its research, to find fresh expressions. The dialectic of this exercise of thought and patience will make us discover elements of truth also in the opinions of others; it will force us to express our teaching with great fairness; and it will reward us for the work of having explained it in accordance with the objectives of another or despite his slow assimilation of our teaching. The dialogue will make us wise.

I believe that many of the contributions to this book will prove helpful in engaging in that dialogue which will make us wise. This book will be particularly helpful to those individuals and groups who care about this issue or whose lives are touched by the human reality and experience of homosexuality. Parents and families, theologians and pastors, women and men religious, vocation and formation personnel, gay and lesbian Catholics will all find in these essays a rich source of stimulating and thought-provoking ideas from writers whose knowledge and experience are invaluable to the People of God. I hope that these essays will help all of us to clarify, revise, or develop our own thinking on the subject of homosexuality. *A Challenge to Love* is a challenge to the whole Church. Some voices challenge us to love and accept homosexual Catholics; some challenge our understanding of human sexuality; some challenge our pastoral approaches. All the voices challenge us, as Christian adults, to engage in the difficult task of providing for gay and lesbian Christians that "special degree of pastoral understanding and care" that we American bishops spoke of in 1976.

What we cannot afford is a failure to meet the challenge to move ahead in our common search for justice. We cannot allow ourselves to be paralyzed by a fear that prevents us from speaking and listening to each other actively, attentively, and respectfully, even at those times when we cannot agree with or accept fully what the other is saying.

The prophet Isaiah said of the Servant, "A bruised reed he shall not break, and a smoldering wick he shall not quench." Jesus never refused dialogue or interaction with any individual or group. He was supremely able to break through all the stereotypes and prejudices of his own age, which categorized and isolated individuals as "poor," "unlearned," "Pharisee," "unclean," "Gentile," "outside the law," and so forth. He was able to reach and touch all such persons with his own healing love, a love which often came in the form of a challenge to listen and hear the voice of God in their lives and respond to that call in even greater trust and fidelity to a loving God who counted the hairs of their heads and cared for them as for the sparrows of the earth. As followers and ministers of that same Jesus, the Church today can do no less.

Walter F. Sullivan
Bishop of Richmond

The Prejudice Against Homosexuals and the Ministry of the Church

Washington State Catholic Conference
Seattle, Washington

April 28, 1983

Introduction

This paper deals with the obligations of authorities in Church and State towards homosexuals. In particular, it focuses upon the nature and the reprehensibleness of the prejudice against such persons in our society and the need to combat such prejudice by policy measures in both Church and State. However, since this paper has been commissioned by Church authorities to represent an official Church position, it does not attempt to rethink or to develop substantially the Catholic position on the morality of homosexuality—however much such rethinking and development is needed in this and all other areas of the Church's tradition. Rather, it presents the current official position as a given for its limited purposes.

At the outset we need to define briefly a few terms. *Orientation* refers to an habitual state of being which inclines one toward certain attitudes and actions. A *homosexual orientation* (some female homosexuals speak of "preference" rather than "orientation") inclines one to prefer as a sexual partner a person of one's own sex. Thus, one is attracted to persons of the same sex and one is more desirous of having genital sex with such persons than with persons of the opposite sex. If such a person engages in genital activity with a person of the same sex, he or she is said to be *acting out homosexually*. This *acting out* is perhaps better called *homogenital activity*. Finally, a *homosexual* (or *homosexual person*) is one who is homosexually oriented, whether he or she acts out or not. A *gay* is a male homosexual; a *lesbian* is a female homosexual; a *straight* person is one who is heterosexual.

Background Elements of the Situation We Face

Two elements constitute the background against which we take up the Catholic principles regulating the obligations of the Church and the State to combat by public measures conditions prejudicial to homosexual persons: (1) the *de facto* conditions of prejudice against gays and lesbians, and (2) the teaching of the Church on homosexuality and prejudice against homosexual persons.

1. PREJUDICE AGAINST HOMOSEXUALS

There is considerable evidence that homosexuals are victims of prejudice. Many in the general population "prejudge" homosexuals in that without evidence they intellectually impute evils such as child molesting to gays and lesbians. Further, because of such prejudgments they often manifest hostile attitudes to homosexuals and act toward them in such a way as to inflict harm upon them, even grave physical harm, simply because they are identified as being homosexual.

The causes of such prejudice are partially known. Some persons fear an orientation and a style of living that differ in important respects from their own. They are gripped by fear of the unknown. Others have received misinformation and prejudicial attitudes from parents and the surrounding environment. In addition, many Christians have based irrational opposition to homosexuals upon a false or fundamentalistic reading of the Scriptures. Within the Catholic Church magisterial teaching has been incorrectly used as a basis for acts against gays and lesbians, and the teaching itself, at times, has been expressed in a way that has occasioned prejudicial attitudes and activity on the part of some Church members.

2. CHURCH TEACHING ON HOMOSEXUALITY AND PREJUDICE AGAINST HOMOSEXUAL PERSONS

a. Church Teaching on the Morality of Homosexual Orientation and Acts

First of all, Church teaching is positive with regard to homosexual persons considered in the totality of their beings. It should be quite obvious that homosexuality is an abstraction. No one is only a homosexual just as no one is only a mother, only a president, or only an artist with no other constituents in her/his makeup. Hence, a homosexual person may manifest virtues and qualities that are admirable by any standard. In fact, there is some evidence that many homosexuals possess important attributes that are often, unfortunately, lacking in their straight counterparts. Thus, it appears that sensitivity to the needs of persons and the ability to express warm feelings towards both men and women are frequently present in gays. Hence, the Church, which considers a person as a whole, can find much good to be praised and affirmed in any homosexual person. Although one's sexuality affects to some extent all that one is and does, just as does every basic quality, homosexual orientation and homosexual acting out constitute but one aspect, and not the most important aspect, of concrete gay and lesbian persons. Accordingly, no matter what one thinks about their homosexuality, one is never justified in labeling such persons as homosexual and then condemning them under that category. No person is merely a category. He or she is composed of many good attributes that outstrip any single category.

Second, Church teaching does not morally condemn homosexual orientation. It is true that it views such an orientation as not fully appropriate since in the person so oriented there is lacking an integration of the psychic side with the procreative possibilities of the physical side. The more a person is integrated, the more he or she unites the physical, the psychological, the intellectual, the volitional and the social. A specific capacity of the physical sex act is to generate a child. An integration of the person implies that the tendency of that person moves him or her toward expressing that physical power in a manner that respects its procreative abilities. Because this integrating tendency is lacking in one homosexually oriented, the Church has traditionally seen such orientation as falling short of the norm of total integration implied in the two great commandments.

However, this inappropriateness of homosexual orientation does not imply that it is sinful in itself or that it is caused by the person's own sin. Although it is apparently true that a small number of lesbians have made a positive choice of their orientation, the evidence seems to indicate that in the vast number of cases homosexuality is not caused by the person but by factors as yet unknown; since the condition is not the result of an individual's free choice, it cannot possibly be the result of personal sin. Instead, it is one of the many results of the human condition that leaves each of us lacking some part of the full integration to which we are called. An older theology spoke of concupiscence and the remains of original sin. Other examples of such remains of original sin are a tendency to anger, inability to commit oneself, inability to communicate with those to whom one is bound, etc. To the degree that such orientations are not caused by the individuals involved, they may not be called sinful. Moral criticism, reproach and blame—if ever they have validity—have validity only with regard to orientations that are freely caused, thoughts and desires that are consented to, and deeds that are freely performed.

Nor are homosexual persons to be blamed for not changing their orientation. It is true that one is obliged to change an habitual orientation which falls short of the ideal insofar as one is able to do so. This is a certain but often forgotten corollary of the two great commandments of the law. However, the best evidence seems to indicate that we have no known way of altering a definite homosexual orientation. To the extent that this continues to be the case, it is unfair and cruel to reproach such persons for not altering or trying to alter their basic condition.

Third, Church teaching is positive about most activities of gays and lesbians. Only homogenital activity and the foreplay to it is disapproved by the Church since it sees these acts as attaining their full significance only in the context of marriage. However, the ordinary acts of life, the expressions of concern and tenderness, the virtues of charity and magnanimity, in short, all that is praised in straight persons is just as much to be accepted, affirmed and praised in homosexual persons. Every other person we know does some kind of activity with which we disagree. Yet, because we recognize that much of their activity is acceptable, we do not condemn globally the actions of such persons. Gays and lesbians have just as much right to our approval and acceptance of their overall activity.

Fourth, Church teaching indicates that even with regard to homogenital activity no one except Almighty God can make certain judgments about the personal sinfulness of acts. This is so because of the conjunction of two factors. On the one hand, each person has unique qualities, unique strengths, and a unique set of weaknesses. Thus, some find it easy to control their tempers and passions; but they are dull, uncreative and little concerned about what is going on about them. Others are inclined to anger and sensuality but they are intensely and creatively interested in the world around them. Each person has a unique starting point for moral living—herself or himself as concretely existing. On the other hand, each person is held to move ever more closely *toward* the ultimate norm of total and integrated love for God, for self, and for every other human person *from where that person happens to be with the strengths and weaknesses that person has*. All specific commandments express aspects of the ideal norm that all are called to—the norm of total love of God and persons. The combination of these two factors indicates that morality has to do with each person's taking the next step toward fulfilling the norm of the two great commandments. A person is guilty of sin only when she or he does not do what she or he is capable of doing in progress toward that norm. Because we cannot know just where another person stands and because we cannot know just how hard that person is trying to live up to the total norm of the two great commandments from where the person is in a given act, we are unable to judge the degree of responsibility the individual bears for the fact that in some aspects his or her act falls short of the moral norm. Thus, we cannot judge the degree of sin involved in a man's failure to grow in his ability to communicate with or show tenderness toward his wife because we do not know just how much he is able to change the present orientation that makes it so difficult for him to share his ideas and tender feelings. In a similar fashion, we cannot judge that a homosexual who engages in homogenital activity is committing subjective sin. What we can say is that this activity falls short of the ultimate norm of Christian morality in the area of genital expression.

b. Church Teaching and Prejudice Against Homosexuals

First of all, prejudice in all its forms falls short of the norm of Christian morality. One can be prejudiced in orientation and attitude, in thought, or in activity. One is prejudiced in orientation and attitude against another person when one's instinctive emotions and interior reactions reject that person or significant aspects of her/his activity with little or no justifying evidence. Thus, to be fearful of some minority person merely because he or she is a minority person or to have a mistrustful attitude toward the teaching ability of all gays or lesbians merely because they are homosexual is to be prejudiced in orientation and attitude. One is prejudiced in thought when without evidence one explicitly thinks evil of another person. Finally, one is prejudiced in activity when one implements in external activity one's prejudicial attitude or thought. *All such forms of prejudice fall short of the Christian norm and must be combatted to the extent possible*. This teaching applies in a special way to gays and lesbians because they have been subjected to prejudice in a gross form.

Second, *the prejudice against homosexuals is a greater infringement of the norm of Christian morality than is homosexual orientation or activity*. A parallel example may illustrate why this is so. Suppose persons who are unable or unwilling to commit themselves, who are incapable of expressing affection toward their spouses, or who are completely insensitive to the needs of others—qualities, by the way, which are frequently destructive of marriage—are labelled "the uncommitted," "those lacking affection," and "the insensitive." Suppose, further, that they are so labelled despite fine qualities they otherwise possess and that they are subjected to indignities solely because of the negative qualities which furnish the basis for the labels they bear. The vast majority of persons would consider such treatment of the uncommitted, the insensitive and the non-affective as grossly prejudicial and immoral. And they would be right. Yet homosexuals are subjected to such treatment merely because they are homosexuals.

Such prejudice hampers homosexual persons in their efforts to grow, makes it easy for them to become embittered at the unfair treatment they experience, and at times leads to their being inflicted with severe bodily injury and even death. Further, such prejudice distorts the personality of the persons who manifest the prejudice, warps their judgment, and leads them to treat other human beings made in the image and likeness of God in a manner that ignores their dignity. The enormity of the moral evil of such prejudice should be obvious.

Third, while the Church's teaching with regard to homosexuality (as outlined above) does not by itself cause prejudice (no more than does its teaching against pre-marital sex cause, by itself, prejudice against unmarried couples who live together), it seems true to say that the manner in which Church teaching has been concretely conveyed has contributed to the prejudice against gays and lesbians. The tendency of some Catholic teachers to speak about homosexual orientation and activity as if these were *the* supreme evils or as if they constituted a dangerous attack on marital values illustrates the point. Further, there have been persons in the Church who have contributed to the general prejudice against homosexuals by the derogatory language and tone they use in referring to gays and lesbians. Finally, many Catholics have heard the Church's teaching against the background furnished by a society whose actions and attitudes are permeated with prejudice against homosexuals. As a result they have given to the Church's teaching a nuance which is prejudicial to homosexual persons.

All this brings out that the Church has a serious obligation with regard to homosexual persons. Because all forms of prejudice are affronts to the dignity of persons, because the prejudice against homosexuals is such a great moral evil, and because Church persons have contributed to the constitution of an environment that is prejudicial to homosexuals, the Church is seriously obliged to work toward the uprooting of such prejudice.

Roles of Church and State in Rectifying this Prejudicial Situation

1. GENERAL CONSIDERATIONS

The Church and the State have partially overlapping and partially different functions in promoting the common good. The State is an agent of public order and it deals only with external situations and activities which affect public peace, public moral existence and justice amidst its citizens. In principle, the State should recognize liberty of thought and should regulate external activity only to the extent that public peace, justice and moral existence would be violated by its failure to act. Hence, the State does not enjoy the role of making judgments on private thoughts or private actions of citizens; nor does it have the function of enjoining its own value system upon its citizens.

The Church also functions in the promotion of the common good of society. Like the State it has a role in the fostering of public order. Thus, the Church has the right and duty to promote laws and situations within the state that foster external order and justice. In addition, the Church is also obligated to care for the public order in its own domain—the parishes, hospitals, and other institutions which it conducts in the carrying out of its mission—by appropriate legislation. In short, both Church and State have a part to play in the regulation of public order. Thus, both have obligations to meet the evil of prejudice insofar as that evil affects the public peace, public moral existence, and justice among those whom they serve.

However, the Church has a further function which it does not share with the State—that of promoting the internalization of the value system inherent in its tradition. This means that is has the right and the duty to inculcate principles of personal and private living and to foster structures that will help enroot these principles in the feelings, attitudes, and activities of its members. Hence, the Church is concerned with more than exterior and public activity; it is concerned with the development of the whole person.

2. SPECIFIC APPLICATIONS TO THE PREJUDICE AGAINST HOMOSEXUALS

a. Applications Pertaining to Church and State

First, the orientation or inclination of any person of itself and apart from any overt activity may not be the basis for depriving him/her of ordinary rights to courtesy, employment, advancement, equal benefits, etc. in either Church or State. Hence, the mere fact that a person has a homosexual orientation is *never* sufficient reason for public discrimination. State and Church authorities have duties to protect these rights of homosexuals. Further, insofar as orientations and inclinations do not of themselves affect the public order, efforts to uncover homosexual tendencies by questionnaires and other investigative techniques are reprehensible.

Second, Church and State authority should see to it that external behavior which is not a matter of public knowledge should not of itself be the basis for discriminating against employees. Should an employer learn of private external behaviors, he/she may not use such information as the basis for terminating or otherwise discriminating against an employee. Only if the behavior in question seriously affects the ability of the person to fulfill the duties of his/her position may a superior discharge him/her. Thus, one may remove an airplane pilot upon discovering that he is frequently drunk on the grounds that he may endanger the lives of passengers. Similarly, if it be true that homosexual intelligence agents are easily subject to blackmail, one may remove them from their posts. The same would hold true for agents involved in any other activities which target them for blackmail.

Third, a person may be disciplined or even discharged from a position if his/her conduct disturbs the just public order. Hence, two homosexuals who make a public display of affection which seriously disrupts a school lunchroom may be dismissed. Two heterosexuals who do the same thing may also be dismissed, and for the same reason—serious disturbance of the public order. However, if the disturbance of order stems more from prejudicial attitudes of the public than from the activity of the homosexual persons, authorities are obligated to do all that is possible to combat such attitudes.

Fourth, all persons are entitled to humane public treatment. Therefore, public authority in Church and State should not allow gays and lesbians, no matter how manifest their lifestyles may be, to be subjected to violence, public insult or scorn, or other public indignities.

In general, individuals have the right to act freely in society as long as they do no harm to others. Public authority should not restrict freedom when such harm does not occur. In fact, it should safeguard such freedom. This is so even if individuals perform acts which others in the society consider immoral. Hence, Catholic theologians have steadfastly opposed laws which punish or restrict private pre-marital sex. To attempt to control such activity by preventative or punitive legislation would lead to invasion of privacy, snooping, and a host of other evils. Similar reasoning applies to homosexual activity of a private nature.

b. Applications which differ from Church to State

The mission of the Church differs from that of the State. Both are obligated to foster the public order, but the Church must also promote the value system that is integral to its mission. To the degree that its value system goes beyond the public order which defines the limits of the State's competence, to that degree will the principles of operation of the Church differ from those of the State.

This means, in the first place, that the Church is obligated to combat, as far as possible, not just manifest prejudice against gays and lesbians but also the underlying prejudicial understandings and attitudes. Jesus came not just to change the activity of persons but to bring about a conversion of heart, mind, and soul as well—in short, a turning of the whole person toward complete love and acceptance of God and every human being, especially the victims of injustice and discrimination. It is not a coincidence that he was found amidst the poor, the despised, the publicans, and the prostitutes. Though we have no explicit record of Jesus' attitude toward homosexuals, we do know that he championed those who were subjected to prejudiced attitudes and behavior in his time.

Secondly, and more concretely, the Church can combat the evil of prejudice against homosexuals by strongly proclaiming the gross evil of prejudicial attitudes and conduct toward lesbians and gays; by fostering legislation at all levels in the State and in the ecclesiastical arena to remove systemic prejudice; by making efforts to purify of all prejudice the manner in which it conveys its moral teaching on homosexuality; by encouraging empirical research on homosexuality and the ways to combat prejudice against lesbians and gays; and by fostering ongoing theological research and criticism, with regard to its own theological tradition on homosexuality, none of which is infallibly taught.

Thirdly, the Church needs to be sensitive to the danger of occasioning prejudice by its manner of implementing its moral position on homosexuality. As we have indicated in the section on *Church Teaching on the Morality of Homosexual Orientation and Acts,* the Church sees such an orientation and such acts as falling short of the norm. Accordingly, the Church is obliged to reflect this in its explicit teaching, in its hiring practices, and in the overall way it projects values.

Hence, the Church has a right to set certain standards of conduct for those who participate in its mission. It has a right and a duty to require that the persons it employs, if they are active homosexuals, neither publicize their lifestyles nor advocate homogenital activity as perfectly acceptable. In other words, it has a right to ask that those who participate in its mission project publicly by word and action its own traditional moral principles. Accordingly, the Church also has a right to dismiss persons who speak against its principles or who so conduct themselves in the public arena that their example gives scandal with regard to these principles. Of course, this in no way means that the Church should not employ homosexuals. Such persons can and should be employed as long as they do nothing to negate the Church's moral position in a serious way. The same can be said for persons who do not live up to the Church's moral norms in other areas. There are no special principles for homosexuals. The Church is obligated to see that they are treated just like other human beings.

By contrast, on the principles we have stated, the State has no business demanding that gays or lesbians project publicly its given set of moral values. Hence, homosexuals who make public their lifestyle or who advocate homosexual orientation and acting out as completely moral should not be excluded from employment as long as their activity does not disrupt the public order. The State should protect them against discrimination occasioned by their lifestyle.

Fourthly, there are a few sensitive issues regarding the employment of homosexuals in Church institutions. Thus, a number of Catholics are concerned about the role of homosexuals in professions which have care of their children. There are those who think that gays and lesbians inevitably impart a homosexual value system to children or that they will molest children. This is a prejudice and must be unmasked as such. There is no evidence that exposure to homosexuals, of itself, harms a child, just as there is no evidence that exposure to couples who live in non-marital unions, of itself, corrupts the young. Accordingly, there is no need to make efforts to screen out all homosexually oriented persons from our educational system. What is to be required is that all those who participate should impart by word and action the Catholic value system. Those who seek employment within the Church can be asked directly if they intend to impart Catholic doctrine and the broad Catholic value system. That is all.

Another problem arises in cases where a Catholic community is rent by deep-seated prejudices against lesbians and gays. In such circumstances it may be impossible to hire homosexuals, even those who do not act out, without having Catholic institutions wrecked or severely hampered in their operation by prejudiced individuals. In such cases those in authority have to balance the harm to the community caused by the destructive activities of these prejudiced persons against the injustice resulting from being pressured not to hire homosexuals or to terminate those already hired. In certain circumstances, those in authority may judge prudentially that they will have to give in to the pressure. In other circumstances, they will prudentially judge that the common good is better fostered by taking a firm stand and braving the wrath of persons blinded by prejudice. Thus prudence in this matter is not to be identified with "playing it safe." Rather, it is to be identified with selecting the best means in ambiguous circumstances of moving toward a greater realization of the common good. No matter what decision is taken, solid efforts must be made to root out such prejudicial attitudes and activities from the community.

Ultimately all people need to be reminded that homosexuals are persons, and, as such, that they have rights and feelings that must be respected. In particular, lesbians and gays have the right and the duty to contribute to society, and they should be encouraged to live up to that right and duty. They are children of God, and they should be treated with all the respect and dignity that children of God deserve. They should be helped by the rest of society to grow toward the wholeness of life revealed in the words and deeds of Jesus.

Ministry and Homosexuality in the Archdiocese of San Francisco

Senate of Priests
San Francisco, California

May, 1983

INTRODUCTION

"Reform your lives and believe in the Good News" (Mark 1:15). This was the central message that Jesus preached to his disciples when he proclaimed the Kingdom of God among us. And this is the central message that the Church continues to proclaim to our world today: a message of challenge, of hope, of unconditional concern. It is the mission and responsibility of the local Church to proclaim this message in all of its fullness to the people of God, and in doing so, to build up a community of faith and love where there is no more Jew or Greek, no more slave or free, but only the freedom and joy that come to the children of God.

The call to discipleship that emerges from the Gospel is the call to conform ourselves to the image and example of Jesus Christ. All of the moral wisdom that is genuinely Christian can be summarized in this: the effort to live as He lived, to serve as He served, to suffer as He suffered. All of us are called to travel this journey together, relying on the aid and support that we can give to one another, and above all, on the help of our God. For we have all too many faults and weaknesses to stand alone. Each of us tries to follow in the footsteps of Jesus Christ, and yet each of us knows well how often we stray from the path of discipleship.

The Church recognizes the difficulties that we encounter in our effort to conform ourselves to Christ in a world that all too often spurns the values of the Gospel. The Fathers of the Second Vatican Council summarized this struggle in these words:

> The modern world shows itself at once powerful and weak, capable of the noblest deed or the foulest. Before it lies the path to freedom or slavery, to progress or retreat, to brotherhood or hatred . . . In man himself, many elements struggle with one another. Thus, on the one hand, as a creature he experiences his limitations in a multitude of ways. On the other hand, he feels himself to be boundless in his desires and summoned to a higher life. Pulled by manifold attractions, he is constantly forced to choose among them and to

> renounce them . . . The Church believes that Christ, who died and was raised for all, can, through his Spirit, offer man the light and strength to measure up to his supreme destiny.[1]

This belief that Christ offers to us the light and strength to follow the path of discipleship is at the core of the mission of the Church. This belief is also the foundation for this pastoral plan on *Ministry and Homosexuality in the Archdiocese of San Francisco*.[2]

It is reputably estimated that there are approximately 120,000 homosexual men and women in the San Francisco Bay Area.[3] Among these men and women there are blacks, whites, Hispanics, Asians, rich, poor, educated, illiterate. There are Democrats, Republicans, independents, old, young, and handicapped. Rich in their diversity, these men and women have one thing in common: They are homosexual, and because of that, their lives have been profoundly affected.[4]

If the Church in San Francisco is to be faithful to its universal salvific mission, it must recognize this fact and ask itself how the presence of this large homosexual population in the Bay Area will influence the effort to make the Archdiocese of San Francisco a true community of faith, a community reflective of the values of the Gospel. This pastoral plan, adopted by the Senate of Priests of the Archdiocese of San Francisco and approved by Archbishop Quinn, is an effort to do just that. This plan is the result of two years of work by a subcommittee of the Senate of Priests, work that has included consultations with homosexual men and women, as well as with theologians, psychologists, and experts in the field of pastoral ministry. As these consultations progressed, it became more and more apparent that any effective pastoral plan must be based upon the teachings of the Church, the "results" of modern social science, and the real lived experiences of homosexual men and women. And above all, it must take into account that, heterosexual or homosexual, we are all called to walk the journey of discipleship together in this world, looking always to the light of Christ for our strength and our guidance.

I. FOUNDATIONS OF MINISTRY

The Holy Spirit, the "Lord and Giver of Life," is present in the Church as the principle of unity, of diversity, and of harmony.

As principle of unity, the Spirit overcomes the divisions of human and cultural origin; as St. Paul explains, we are "all one in Christ Jesus," and thus there is "neither Jew nor Greek, there is neither male nor female" (Galatians 3:28).

As principle of diversity, the Spirit gives a variety of gifts for the common good of the Church, for the upbuilding of the Body of Christ. The Spirit gives to each for the benefit of all. The Pauline lists (e.g., 1 Corinthians 12:1-31), then, should be regarded as illustrative rather than exhaustive. It is here that we find the essence of ministry in the Church: the gift of the Spirit is to be exercised for the upbuilding of the Church: "To each is given the manifestation of the

Spirit for the common good" (1 Cor 12:7).

As principle of harmony, the Spirit draws together and orders these various gifts. It is here that we find the object of the Church's ministry: to order and harmonize the gifts of all.

The Church's ministry, therefore, always seeks the goal of unity, a goal which calls for harmony, which preserves the diversity of gifts and orders them toward unity.

One area of concern that the Church in the Archdiocese of San Francisco seeks to touch is the complex arena of homosexuality. In this Holy Year of Redemption, the Senate of Priests is very cognizant of the Pope's affirmation concerning Christian unity, "a reciprocal harmony of intent in all who believe in Christ . . ."

In his *Pastoral Letter on Homosexuality* of 5 May 1980, Archbishop Quinn stated that "The Church recognizes the complexity of the question (of homosexuality) as it exists in the life of an individual person . . . There must be sensitivity in treating the question. Homosexual persons must be helped and encouraged to strive for wholeness and personal integrity . . ." (20-21).

Homosexuality is, then, truly a complex issue, in both its personal and social dimensions. The subject must be treated with great care and understanding, a treatment rooted in the Church's teachings about morality and the human meaning of sexuality.

In the search for unity, we must constantly remember that morality is first of all a call to conform our lives to the image of Jesus Christ. St. Paul names Christ as "the image of the Invisible God, the first-born of all creatures. In Him everything in heaven and on earth was created . . . In Him, everything continues in being" (Col 1:15-17).

Christian morality is, then, not arbitrary; rather it is the faithful articulation in our lives of the image of Jesus Christ. The fundamental ethical command imposed on the Christian is the imitation of Christ, which means seeking to be as faithful to the human vocation as He was.

The Church's ministry to homosexual people must proceed knowledgeably. There have been multiple studies published about homosexuality, some of which have given particular attention to the homosexual communities in San Francisco.[5]

These studies raise a variety of concerns, attitudes and conclusions. What does seem clear, however, is that the homosexual orientation is not simply a matter of moral weakness or sinful indulgence or a truncated sexual development. While these factors might be present in some persons, it seems false and misinformed to conclude that all homosexual men and women suffer from such anomalies of behavior.

The Church sustains a long history of sexual morality, based on its understanding of Scriptural principles, human nature and theological reflection. The principles of this sexual morality are clear: all men and women are called to live chastely outside of marriage and to live chastely in exclusive love with one's spouse in marriage.

The Church rejects the concept that sexual activity is neutral or that homosexual activity is objectively good. This rejection doubtlessly creates great tensions for many people, especially those persons who do, in fact, sustain a homosexual orientation.

It is precisely because of such tensions that the Church's ministry is so very important. Homosexual people should never be treated with ridicule, contempt or hatred. On the contrary, as the Bishops of this country affirmed in their 1976 pastoral letter, *To Live in Christ Jesus,* homosexual people must be treated with understanding, patience and love, and should never be the object of prejudice on the basis of their sexual orientation.

The Church is quite aware of the fact that it is not easy to live chastely, especially when one does not have the support of married life or the inspiration of vows or a celibate commitment made in the midst of a faith community.

What, then, are homosexual Catholics looking for from the Church's ministry? As all Catholics, they look to the Church for a community in which the Gospel can be lived and their spiritual lives can be enriched. They look to the Church for support for their Christian faith and their Catholic heritage. They seek an understanding Church, a community where they can be accepted as men and women who are Catholic and who also happen to be homosexual. They look to the Church as a community of faith, a place where they may responsibly and sensitively understand the interplay between their religious faith and their human sexuality, and to live the sacramental life of the Church in all of its rich meanings.

St. Paul urges, in his second letter to the Corinthians, that Christians ". . . agree with one another, live in peace; and the God of love and peace will be with you" (13:11-12).

While the scriptural context of this passage is undoubtedly liturgical, Paul's admonition is likewise a challenge to all Christians to openly and honestly manifest their faith in Jesus Christ.

The Senate of Priests desires to help foster a supportive atmosphere where all Christians might live in peace, harmony and unity. The Senate thus presents this paper in the hope of creating a more viable ministry in this local Church to and for homosexual people.

Personhood and Homosexuality: Counseling the Homosexual Person: 1

1. The Feelings of a Homosexual Person.

Any ministry to homosexual people must begin with an attempt deeply to appreciate the feelings that lie within the individual man and woman. A recent study commissioned by the Commission on Social Justice of the Archdiocese of San Francisco (July 1982) gives a number of concrete examples where homosexual people have felt profoundly hurt and mistreated by the Church. These feelings cannot be discarded and ridiculed.

Many homosexual persons were interviewed by the subcommittee of the Senate of Priests in the course of the two years this paper has been in the process of research and formulation.

It is clear to us that the examples given in the study mentioned above are not isolated or exaggerated. Numerous homosexual Catholics feel that the behavior of homosexual people is judged more seriously than that of heterosexual people. Homosexual Catholics often state that they feel that the Church regards their orientation and behavior as the *peccatum pessimum,* the worst type of sinful conduct.

At the same time, this awareness does not match the experience of many homosexual people. In other words, they do not experience their homosexual orientation as sinful, truncated or abnormal.

It is clear that one of the worst burdens that many homosexual people sustain is the *feeling* outwardly of being taboo, while inwardly sensing a rightness about their sexuality. The human dilemma here is obvious: the homosexual person feels rejected by society and the Church, and thus for all practical purposes, feels that the fact of a homosexual orientation is, in itself, a sin. The Church's ministry to homosexual people must begin with these deep *feelings* and move in such a direction that homosexuality might be a building block rather than a stumbling block in the ongoing search for unity and harmony.

2. What it Means to be "Different."

This feeling of ambiguity creates in the homosexual person an awareness of being "different" from the majority of people. This consciousness of being different, of belonging to a minority, leaves the homosexual person suffering from the same type of problem as other persons who sense themselves to be in a minority, with the added but important factor that their "difference" often must be a secret one. This need for secrecy can lead to a deeper alienation.

Ministry to homosexual people must, likewise, recognize that this "difference" is greatly at the heart of society's treatment of homosexual people as objects of cruel jokes and contempt. This "objectification" then leads the homosexual person to feelings of a lack of self-esteem and loneliness. In ordinary mixed society, then, homosexual people often feel like strangers. They are shunned and despised, while knowledge about them is very often greatly distorted.

While it may be true that some homosexual people use this "difference" to sustain a subculture where persons are reduced to objects and sexuality is totally divorced from one's total humanity, a large number of homosexual people continue to look to the Church for a place where they might identify authentic human integrity and holiness of life. The vulgar exhibitionism that we see too often in some parts of the city of San Francisco and inscribed blatantly in a number of gay newspapers and magazines should not keep the Church from developing a sound ministry to homosexual people who are sincerely striving for integrity of life.

Many good people who are homosexual are constantly struggling against the pressures of the homosexual subculture; these people must be assisted not to despair, and the Church must offer them encouragement and support. Rejection by the Church and its pastors might push homosexual persons to rely exclusively on a subculture that demeans them and violates their personal integrity.

Most professionals would agree that the homosexual persons sustain a psychic constitution that orients them toward a same-sexed psychological, emotional and erotic structure. The true homosexual is usually aware of this orientation at a very early age, if not explicitly, at least implicitly, with the feeling of being different.

Ministry to homosexual people must proceed, then, with an awareness that the homosexual person *is* different and has not *chosen* this difference. Homosexuality appears to be a condition deeply imbedded in an individual long before any conscious choice is made.

3. What Homosexuality Does Not Mean.

Whatever the elements, whatever the blend, most homosexual adults have no awareness of having *chosen* homosexuality. In early adolescence when others' fantasies focused on the opposite sex, theirs focused on the same sex. In later adolescence and early adulthood when others fell in and out of love with the opposite sex, they fell in and out of love with the same sex. When others committed themselves in the context of the lifelong companionship of marriage, the homosexual person often had only the bar, "the closet," and personal isolation.

In some unrecountable manner, something "different" had happened to shape the homosexual person's development during the early critical years of childhood.

Crucial to this realization is the significant acknowledgement that a person's homosexuality should not be translated as a "master trait:" that is, a person should not be reduced to his or her homosexual orientation. A homosexual person may, in fact, be well-adjusted or maladjusted, promiscuous or unpromiscuous, religious or irreligious, reliable or unreliable.

In society, the label "homosexual " often places people in a category of misfits, an excluded deviant class, a category that then leads to a host of misinformation and exaggerations about homosexual people; and ultimately to violence.

Misinformation and categorical definitions usually lead to the belief that homosexual persons are inferior and may then be mistreated with impunity, prejudice and violent action. This general conviction is commonly expressed in such prejudices as: by definition, homosexual persons are child molesters, oversexed and licentious characters. There is no reputable data whatsoever that supports this type of conclusion, and ministry to the homosexual person must acknowledge this fact.

At least these points must be recognized:

(a) It is untrue that most homosexual persons are attracted to children and adolescents;

(b) It is inaccurate that most homosexual people are easily identified;

(c) It is misleading to say that most homosexual people automatically recognize each other;

(d) It is untrue that homosexual people are automatically unstable and promiscuous;

(e) It is a misunderstanding to claim that homosexual people simply need will-power to correct their orientation;

(f) It is inaccurate to identify all homosexual people with radical pressure groups;

(g) It is incorrect to assert that homosexual persons sustain a higher incidence of mental disorder; and

(h) It is inaccurate to assume that homosexual persons are limited to only certain social classes or professions.

As we become more cognizant of these factors, we will hopefully become more understanding of the meaning of the Catholic Bishops when they counselled in *To Live in Christ Jesus* (1976): "Homosexuals, like everyone else, should not suffer from prejudice against their basic human rights; they have a right to respect, friendship, and justice. They should have an active role in the Christian community." This same counsel is gathered from the many homosexual people we interviewed and the literature we studied: the homosexual person seeks from the Church a sensitive attitude, where he or she might be allowed to *be* homosexual: that is, a Church where he or she will find acceptance, understanding and love.

The Call of Holiness: Counseling the Homosexual Person: 2

In his work, *On Flight,* St. Ambrose writes: "The life we live is not now our ordinary life but the life of Christ: a life of sinlessness, of chastity, of simplicity and every other virtue. We have risen with Christ. Let us live in Christ, let us ascend in Christ . . ."

Christian morality is primarily concerned about this call to live "the life of Christ," this holiness of life. We must never forget that we are all under the grace of God, and with grace, all things are possible.

Fundamental to all ministry to homosexual people is this need to administer the resources of grace for true and authentic transformation of life.

Accordingly, the Church must seek to fulfill certain exigencies that will assist the homosexual person to realize deeply his or her call to holiness of life:

(a) To provide a preaching and teaching ministry where we are confronted with the biblical truth of the all holy God who seeks in Jesus and in the Church to release persons from sin and hatred; it is God who moves the heart toward true repentance;

(b) To provide a preaching and teaching ministry that emphasizes God's call to spiritual renewal, the need for zeal in both personal and social dimensions of morality, and the power of the Spirit to transform our lives; and

(c) To provide a preaching and teaching ministry that stresses the grace and power for renewal available in prayer and in the sacramental life of the Church.

The power of sin remains virulent in our world and affects both personal and social structures. To model ourselves in the image of Jesus Christ clearly demands a deep prayer life and a participation in the sacraments of the Church, especially Reconciliation and the Eucharist.

St. Paul enjoins us in Romans 12:12 to "Rejoice in your hope, be patient in tribulation, be constant in prayer." We will not reach perfection in the love of neighbor if that love does not rise from love of God as its root.

In his *Pastoral Letter on Homosexuality,* Archbishop Quinn has written:

> ". . . in the Eucharist and in the Sacrament of Penance supported by a life of daily prayer and growing faith, every believer finds that what is judged impossible by the world is indeed possible" (p. 24).

Homosexual people have the same need for the sacraments as heterosexual people; and they have the same right to receive the sacraments. Two of the elements that clearly exclude a person from receiving the Eucharist are: a lack of personal faith; and the commitment to or awareness of personal, serious sin.

The Catholic Bishops of England and Wales have addressed this fact directly in their 1981 letter, *An Introduction to the Pastoral Care of Homosexual People:*

> "In determining whether or not to administer Absolution or give Communion to a homosexual, a pastor must be guided by the general principles of fundamental theology that only a certain moral obligation may be imposed. An invincible doubt, whether of law or fact, permits one to follow a true and solidly 'probable opinion' in favor of a more liberal interpretation" (p. 13).

The specific meaning of this directive becomes clear as we carefully consider the importance of the following three points:

1. The Principle of Gradualism

To live an authentic life of holiness and prayer calls for a deep personal conversion, a conversion that oftentimes necessitates gradual change and development. This principle of gradualism is consistent with the Church's moral tradition[6] and finds a clear articulation in Pope John Paul II's *Apostolic Exhortation on the Family* (November 1981):

> "What is needed is a continuous, permanent conversion which, while requiring an interior detachment from every evil and an adherence to good in its fullness, is brought about concretely in steps which lead us ever forward. Thus, a dynamic process develops, one which advances gradually with the progressive integration of the gifts of God and the demands of His definitive and absolute love in the entire personal and social life of man" (n. 9).[7]

John Paul II nuanced this principle in his Address to the College of Cardinals on 5 November 1979. He was speaking of the whole community of the Church and the need we all must sustain toward "solidarity with these brothers and sisters in the faith . . ." He then adds:

> "Solidarity means above all a proper understanding and then proper action, not on the basis of what corresponds to the concept of the person offering help, but on the basis of what corresponds to the real needs of the person being helped, and what corresponds to his or her dignity."

The principle of gradualism thus recognizes that personal movement toward greater good and deeper personal integrity is gradual and progressive and is brought about only "in steps." Every minister in the Church must carefully discern this "dynamic process" within the "person being helped." Ministry within the Catholic Church can never ignore the Church's ethical teachings on human sexuality and the objective immorality of homosexual activity.

Concomitantly, however, it is likewise important to carefully interpret the meaning of sexual activity in this person's life: that is, to understand the pattern of life in which such activity takes place and to take into consideration the meaning that these sexual acts have for different people.

Pope Paul VI affirmed this same principle of gradualism on 8 December 1974 in his Exhortation on "The Holy Year and Reconciliation in the Church." The Pope urged every individual "to look critically at himself and his actions" so that he may be led "to more prudent choices." He then counsels:

> "We exhort all the faithful . . . 'carefully to examine the innermost places of your heart and explore the recesses of your soul' . . . For the Spirit is present and active in the depths of every Christian soul, leading all in humility and peace along the paths of truth and love . . . We greatly desire . . . that the whole people of God would advance . . . on . . . the stages of sanctification."

The 1973 document of the Catholic Bishops, *Principles To Guide Confessors in Questions of Homosexuality,* recognizes this same principle of gradualism. In speaking of the need for homosexual persons to develop stable relationships, this document teaches:

> "If a homosexual has progressed . . . in the effort to develop a stable relationship with a given person (but) has *occasionally* fallen into . . . sin, he should be absolved and instructed to take measures to avoid the sin without breaking off a friendship which has helped him grow as a person" (p. 11).

There is a clear recognition here that personal integrity comes about progressively and an attitude of support and encouragement is the "proper action" that must be taken.

For the many reasons we have already mentioned, many homosexual people find their lives to be lonely and their sexuality to be a burden. While this is not so in all cases, it is a fact in many instances. It is this need for closeness and intimacy that leads the homosexual person to seek stable relationship with another person. Homosexual people fall in love. And as long as this is so, sexual activity might occasionally occur.

Objectively, the Church teaches that homosexual activity in such unions, or in any situation, is morally unacceptable. The principle of gradualism recognizes this fact and assists the person toward a progressive assimilation of the Church's ethical values. Pastoral judgments can never be made in the abstract, therefore, but always within the concrete circumstances of this person's life.

The 1975 document of the Sacred Congregation for the Doctrine of the Faith, *Declaration on Certain Questions Concerning Sexual Ethics,* makes this same point:

> "It is true that in sins of the sexual order, in view of their kind and their causes, it more easily happens that true consent is not fully given; this is a fact which calls for caution on all judgments as the subject's responsibility."

Ministry in this area thus demands an awareness that purification and growth in holiness come about only gradually. Instant serenity is almost never the human reality. Every person of faith must cope with his or her personal sinfulness and human limitations. These vary from person to person and are frequently complex and discouraging; but all persons, even in spite of limitations and even failure, must continue to grow in holiness of life.

This principle of gradualism has roots within the scriptural ethical tradition[8] where there is, on the one hand, an awareness of human sinfulness and, on the other hand, a recognition of the inexhaustible vastness of God's love and grace. Any failure, then, to totally realize at this moment everything that one is called to be and to do does not negate the possibility of future success. We are all sinners who at times violate our best moral convictions, but we can be healed and forgiven.

2. The Role of Conscience

In setting before homosexual men and women this call to perfection, the Church also reminds them of the need to *personally* respond to this call, and central to this response is the role of their properly formed conscience.

The proper formation of conscience necessitates both a learning of moral rules and a personal internalization of the Christian principles inherent in the truths that Christ revealed.

The Church's moral tradition has made important distinctions among various degrees of conscience formation: e.g., between a correctly formed and an incorrectly formed conscience. These moral distinctions are best understood as a spectrum, as it is possible for a person to sustain correct formation in one area of morality and incorrect formation in another.

One type of conscience often experienced today, which is not properly formed in light of the Church's ethical teachings, is the belief which claims that, since homosexuality is a deep and integral component of a person's psychic structure, it is virtually impossible for such people to lead lives of chastity. Such approaches often argue that the stability of a homosexual union outweighs the objective disorder of homosexual activity.

This type of conscience likewise maintains that since the homosexual orientation seems to be normative for at least a certain number of people in society, homosexual activity must be judged as normal and good for these people.

This type of conscience fails to grasp and integrate the Church's teaching that all sexual activity finds its best and morally good expression only within the context of the man-woman covenanted relationship of marriage.

At another end of the conscience spectrum are persons who sustain a scrupulous conscience. These people regard every single homosexual act as a serious sin because of the offense against chastity, without due consideration of the predisposition of the subject, or the pressures and tensions that have traditionally been understood to mitigate personal culpability.

Ministry to homosexual people who might find themselves to be unnecessarily scrupulous in the moral evaluation of their sexual activity needs to help these people better assess the wholeness and integrity of their lives. It is precisely because of this need that the Church desires to extend to homosexual men and women its resources for spiritual direction and personal counseling.

While the Church teaches that homosexual activity is objectively inconsistent with the meaning of human sexuality, it never wants to evaluate this activity totally divorced from the person or circumstances in which the activity takes place. It is one thing to consider homosexual acts from an objective perspective; it is quite another reality to judge individual homosexual people and their subjective culpability in the face of pressures and the possible loneliness which they experience.

The importance of individual conscience is attested to in the *Dogmatic Constitution on the Church* of Vatican Council II:

> "In the depths of his conscience, man detects a law which he does not impose upon himself, but which holds him to obedience. Always summoning him to love good and avoid evil, the voice of conscience can, when necessary, speak to his heart more specifically: do this, shun that . . .
>
> Conscience is the most secret core and sanctuary of a man. There he is alone with God, whose voice echoes in his depths . . . (T)he more that a correct conscience holds sway, the more persons and groups turn aside from blind choice and strive to be guided by objective norms of morality.
>
> Conscience frequently errs from invincible ignorance without losing its dignity . . ." (n.16).

Clearly, then, the Church upholds the inviolable dignity of personal conscience, but recognizes at the same time that individual conscience needs guidance and formation in order to foster a correct conscience.

Ministry to homosexual people must acknowledge, therefore, the sanctity of conscience, but must also assist persons toward a formation of conscience that is guided by the "objective norms of morality." Sensitive pastoral expertise is thus called for to assist a homosexual person to respect his or her own individual "secret core" while also being attentive to and responsive toward the norms of sexual and personal morality taught in the scriptures and the tradition of the Church.

3. The Responsibility of Chastity.

Genesis 1:31 tells us that God saw all of creation as "very good," a view which is grounded in the belief that human sexuality is likewise good, a gift from God. Chastity is a virtue of responsibility: by it we strive to live out our human sexuality to the fullness of its human potential. As the *Declaration on . . . Sexual Ethics* teaches, chastity "increases the human person's dignity and enables one to love truly, disinterestedly, unselfishly and with respect for others" (n. 12). This call to perfection through a life of chastity is addressed to all people, whether their orientation is heterosexual or homosexual, single or married.

The homosexual orientation is not held to be a sinful condition; as with heterosexuality, it represents the situation in which one finds oneself, the starting point for one's response to Christ's call to perfection. Responding to this call does not mean that one must change this orientation. Rather, it entails living out the demands of chastity within that orientation.

This call to live chastely is a challenge that many people today disregard and even ridicule. It is, thus, of utmost importance that we remember always our moral tradition that in Jesus "we have reccived grace" (Romans 1:5) and thus has our "old self" been crucified; we are indeed "under grace" (Romans 6:14).

The power of sin makes itself evident so that we do not always actualize the norms and details to which Christ and the Church call us. Homosexual men and women, authentically struggling with the difficult tension between orientation and sexual behavior must always be met, then, with understanding, patience and love.

Chastity means the *responsible* expression of one's sexuality, a free response to God's grace. Chastity is a virtue of the sexual self whereby discipline is combined with heart-felt celebration. As a Christian virtue, it is the enemy of any type of personal narcissism and every irresponsible gesture of relatedness. It always moves one to seek a fitting correspondence between meaning and act; it says: we are sexual beings, but we are also more besides, and sexual expression must serve the purposes of the whole self before God.

The Church encourages heterosexual people to live chaste lives as married/unmarried, as widows/widowers, as separated and/or divorced persons. The Christian community has a stake in preserving the symmetry of this ethical demand in the situation of both heterosexual and homosexual people.

It is clearly a better moral situation for two homosexual people to live together chastely in a permanent supportive relationship than to seek out partners indiscriminately and promiscuously. This option "to live together chastely in a permanent supportive liaison" is consistent with the *Principles To Guide Confessors in Questions of Homosexuality* (1973).

These *Principles* counsel a confessor to "encourage the (homosexual) person to form relationships with persons of both sexes" (p. 9) and to sustain "the formation of a stable friendship with at least one person" (p. 11).

Consistent with the principle of gradualism, the *Principles* recognize the need for deep prayer to sustain such a relationship and acknowledge that occasionally instances of sexual activity might occur. If this activity is truly "occasional," and the persons are sincerely attempting to live lives of chaste love and commitment, ". . . he or she should be absolved" and instructed on how one might avoid homosexual activity "without breaking off a friendship that has helped him grow as a person" (p. 11).

Chastity is always the responsibility and the goal of the Christian life; it is a virtue achieved with perfection only as we rely fully on God's grace. The *Principles* thus realize that the homosexual person "should not be surprised by periodic tensions and some relapses" (p. 15).

Pastoral Conclusions

As noted above in *An Introduction to the Pastoral Care of Homosexual People* by the Bishops of England and Wales, ministry to homosexual people necessitates careful discernment in determinations about sacramental participation. The minister should be guided in this determination by a sensitive discernment of the homosexual person's assimilation of the values enunciated here under the titles of the principle of gradualism, the role of conscience, and the responsibility of chastity.

II. MINISTRY TO THE HOMOSEXUAL COMMUNITIES

In light of these foundations for ministry, it is clear that the Archdiocese of San Francisco must develop and support effective methods for ministering to the homosexual communities in the Bay Area. Many homosexual men and women in the Archdiocese are Catholic, and many look to the Church as a source of guidance and support in their lives. To ignore the spiritual needs of these men and women, or to ignore the particular needs posed by their homosexuality, is to ignore the example of Christ who knew no barriers to his ministry but reached out to all people with the hand of love.

For this reason, the Archdiocese of San Francisco has an obligation to establish ministerial structures that touch in a special way the lives of homosexual men and women. These structures should be several and should be diverse; for they must touch the lives of people who are diverse in all but their sexual orientation. Yet different as these structures are, they must have the following characteristics:

a. They must signal that homosexual persons are children of God and are full members of the Church who add to its richness and vitality by their lives;

b. They must not undermine the normative teaching of the Church that homosexual activity is wrong;

c. While separate from other ministries, these structures must enhance the unity of the whole Church in the Archdiocese; and

d. No one of these structures should attempt to be *the* ministry for homosexual men and women. Each should recognize that homosexual men and women will need and benefit from various types of ministry.

Keeping in mind these principles, it is recommended that the Archbishop establish four primary models of ministry to homosexual persons in the Archdiocese of San Francisco: ministry in the parish; ministry in spiritual support groups; ministry in organizations of Catholic homosexual men and women; and individual ministry to the alienated.

1. Ministry in the Parish.

On 5 May 1981, Archbishop Quinn gave a major address to the priests of the Archdiocese of San Francisco in which he evaluated the life of the local Church. The central theme of that address, which has become a foundation for pastoral action in the Archdiocese, is that the center and primary focus for all of the work of the local Church is the life of the parish: "It is in the parish that we find by far the greatest number of our people. And it is in the parish that they, in turn, most closely encounter the Church. And it is through the parish that they become more and more perfectly Church." Thus, all of the programs and activities of the Archdiocese must be seen in light of the parish. This is no less true for the efforts of the local Church to minister effectively to its large homosexual populations.

For this reason, the most important place where homosexual ministry will occur is in the parish. And for this reason, we must work to insure that all of the parishes in the Archdiocese are communities of faith where homosexual men and women will feel welcome, where they will see themselves as genuinely an important part of the Church.

It will be objected by some that the ministry of the parish is too diverse to be effective in creating a welcoming and ministering climate for homosexual men and women. But this is to miss the point that the elements that are essential to making a parish appealing for homosexual persons are the very same things that are essential to making a parish appealing to heterosexual persons. These include fostering a spirit of faith, service and self-sacrifice. They also include working toward a spirit of warmth, of hospitality, of compassion and understanding. By building a family of faith centered upon the values of the Gospel, the pastor and staff of a parish will also be building a community where all people, regardless of their sexual orientation, will encounter the face of Christ. The Archdiocese is fortunate to have many pastors and staffs eagerly working toward that goal.

In addition to those activities that are directed toward the general welfare of the parish, pastors and staffs should take specific steps to make homosexual men and women feel welcome.[9] The special concerns of homosexual persons that violence and prejudice should not be directed against anyone because of sexual orientation should be embodied in parish social justice activities. Preaching should stress the dignity of all people, whether heterosexual or homosexual. Through small but important steps such as these, the parish can be an effective form of ministry to our homosexual brothers and sisters and can reinforce in all of us the need to walk with one another in seeking the path of Christ.

2. Ministry in Spiritual Support Groups.

While the parish is the focal point for ministry to homosexual men and women in the Archdiocese of San Francisco, there must also be complementary specialized ministries to homosexual Catholics. One very effective method of undertaking such a ministry has been developed by Father John Harvey, O.S.F.S., Father Vincent Serps, O.P., and others. It is a well-conceived cursus of group spiritual support that assists homosexual persons in the goal of coming closer to Christ in their lives.[10]

In this method of group spiritual direction, members of each group meet at least once a week for a two-hour period. The first hour of the evening is spent in prayer: meditation before the Blessed Sacrament, Biblical reflection, or sharing the Eucharist. The second hour of each session is spent in substantive dialogue about the events that have occurred in the participants' lives since the previous meeting. The dialogue is frank, open, and honest, and it is carried on always within the context of the belief that God is the preeminent source of strength in our lives. The goal of these sessions is to enable homosexual men and women to form relationships that are intimate and life-giving, yet totally chaste.

The group meeting is the core of this method of spiritual growth, but it is not the only element. Each participant is also asked to formulate a personal plan of life, an individualized program that will allow him or her to live out a Christ-like life during the whole of the week. These plans must include prayer, the performance of apostolic and charitable works, and regular individualized spiritual direction. The life plan must also assist the individual in developing strong outside friendships, so that the support group does not become an isolating force. Finally, the life-plan must include the frequent reception of the sacraments and ongoing participation in the life of the whole Church.

This structure of group spiritual direction offers a fine model of ministry to a significant number of Catholics. It witnesses to the Gospel and the teachings of the Church. In emphasizing the call to conversion which is common to all while simultaneously acknowledging the special situations of homosexual men and women, this method takes seriously the sexuality of homosexual persons while not presenting it as the primary element in their being. The group model also serves to create a community of deep and growing faith that will assist participants in their effort to grow in the Lord.

For these reasons, we urge that the Archbishop take steps to encourage the formation of numerous spiritual support groups based upon this model. In selecting priests and others to lead such groups, he should seek persons who are trained in spiritual direction, lead deep lives of prayer, and have the sensitivity to minister openly and effectively to homosexual men and women.

3. Organizations of Catholic Homosexual Men and Women.

We realize that for many homosexual men and women who are seeking a specialized ministry from the Church, such intensive spiritual support groups will not constitute a realistic avenue of personal development. It is for this reason that several large organizations of Catholic homosexual men and women have been founded in San Francisco in recent years. Many Catholics have found in these organizations a pathway that has brought them closer to Christ and the Church. For many, the values of responsibility and human dignity fostered in these organizations have been their salvation amid a culture that adulates promiscuity.

Recognizing this, we call upon the Archdiocese to support in these organizations those elements that enhance and further the values of the Gospel. Specifically, this should include assisting these organizations in their efforts to fight homophobia, encouraging them in their goals of promoting personal responsibility and commitment, and helping them to gain access to Church facilities for meetings. In addition, the Archdiocese should encourage the priests and sisters who work with these organizations to vividly signal the Church's ongoing interest in the spiritual and social lives of their members. In doing this, priests and religious should always be faithful to the teachings of the Church.

The Archdiocese should also develop clear lines of communication with the major organizations of Catholic homosexual men and women. This would not only allow a greater collaboration with these organizations on the issues of human rights and personal responsibility, but would also prevent some of the misunderstandings that have occurred in the past. This communication role should be carried on by the Board of Ministries outlined below.

4. Individual Ministry to the Alienated.

It is a tragic, but nonetheless very evident fact, that many fine homosexual men and women are alienated from the Church. In some cases, this has resulted from individual incidents with priests, sisters, brothers, and lay people that have left scars and resentment. In other cases, this alienation has arisen from the tension-filled crises of faith that are common to people of all sexual orientations, but which are compounded by homosexual identity. In many cases, this alienation has arisen from difficulties with or misunderstandings about the teachings of the

Church. But whatever its origins, this alienation from Church that is so present among many homosexual Catholics is a serious pastoral problem that must be addressed.

The Archdiocese of San Francisco has for several years been attempting to deal with the general problem of alienation from the Church. In large part, this effort has taken place in the parishes, where many outstanding priests, sisters, and lay people have undertaken this vital work of healing the scars and misunderstandings. But this work has also been complemented in recent years by official outreach programs of the Archdiocese that attempt to reconcile alienated Catholics with the Church. A great deal of work done by these programs has been with homosexual men and women.

We encourage the work of the Archdiocese in developing new methods of reaching out to alienated Catholics, many of whom are homosexual. We urge that parishes be particularly aware of the need for this vital ministry of reconciliation. We further urge that the Archdiocese provide increased funding for the ministry to the alienated and further explore areas, such as detention ministry and ministries to street people where alienated Catholics of all sexual orientations might be reached. For certainly we, like Jesus himself, must go out and proclaim the message of God's salvation to those in our streets as well as those in our churches.

5. Board of Ministries.

There are two themes that are fundamental to this section on ministry to homosexual men and women. The first is that the Archdiocese must develop an effective and comprehensive ministry to its homosexual people. The second is that no single form of ministry can effectively serve the diversity of homosexual men and women in the Archdiocese of San Francisco. In designing an over-arching structure to coordinate and expand ministry to homosexual persons in the Archdiocese, both of these principles, must be kept in mind.

For this reason, we urge the Archbishop to establish a Board of Ministries to Homosexual Men and Women in the Archdiocese. The goal of this board would be to develop, coordinate, and support a variety of ministries to homosexual persons. These should include parish ministry, ongoing spiritual support groups, organizations of Catholic homosexual men and women, and a strong outreach to the alienated. These ministries should also include whatever further lines of development may surface in the Board's efforts to make the Church present to our homosexual brothers and sisters.

The membership of the Board should be appointed by the Archbishop from among individuals who are involved in ministry to homosexual persons. It should include such representative groups as pastors, priests, sisters, and brothers, as well as representative lay people, who work with homosexual men and women.

The Board should meet approximately once a month and should forward policy recommendations to the Secretariat for Pastoral Ministry and to the Archbishop.

The Board should also have the overall responsibility for implementing new policies designed to foster ministry to homosexual men and women.

III. MINISTRY TO THE WHOLE BELIEVING COMMUNITY

Homosexual men and women, it has been seen, are confronted with a complex and difficult challenge because of their sexual orientation. But the challenge presented by homosexuality is not limited to homosexual persons. Rather homosexuality presents all people with a challenge to grow in toleration, openness, and mutual understanding. As members of the Church, we profess to seek a unity under the headship of Jesus Christ, a unity where the divisions of race, faith, and ethnic background will disappear. If we are to be faithful to the full message of the Gospel, then this unity must also embrace people of all sexual orientations, for the God who is Father of all, desires for us a unity that knows no barriers.

But such a unity will not come suddenly, and must not be achieved by undermining the teachings of the Gospel and of the Church. The healing of the human spirit will take many years and will come only with much struggle and with the aid of God. But the Church has a responsibility to work toward that unity in our world, and for that reason, the Church must undertake a ministry regarding homosexuality to the whole believing community.

Such a ministry must bring to the entire community a sense of what it is like to be homosexual, to feel the alienation, the hurt, the prejudice that are so intimately tied to the experience of being homosexual in our society. Such a ministry must also bring before the people of God the denial of legitimate human and social rights, which is all too pervasive, and the unconscionable acts of violence that are directed against homosexual men and women because of their orientation. This ministry of the Church to all believers must remind us that Christ identified closely with the marginal members of society, with those whom society called outcasts. And we must be reminded, also, that whenever we direct hatred or slurs or violence against one of these homosexual brothers or sisters of Christ, we are directing it against the Lord himself.

In short, the whole believing community must come to appreciate the oppressive walls that have been and are being erected to cut us off from our homosexual brothers and sisters. And we must work together on all sides of those walls to tear them down, inch by inch, until the barriers of anger and misunderstanding and fear that divide us exist no more.

Preaching.

A vital part of this ministry to the whole believing community regarding homosexuality involves preaching in Sunday and weekday homilies. The texts of the Scriptures are filled with rich passages emphasizing the need for tolerance, understanding, and deepest charity among believers. Jesus in his own life consistently condemned those who looked down upon people because they were different, and he chastised those who labeled some of God's children unclean. Many of the stories of the Old Testament reveal experiences of pain, of alienation, of prejudice, and hatred. By using these passages and applying them to the present day, priests and deacons can convey to their people something of the experience of being homosexual in our society. And in doing this, they will be helping to break down the barriers of fear and ignorance that so often separate our communities of faith.

Two examples are included below to indicate how such exegesis might take place:

1. Isaiah 56: 3-5

Let not the foreigner who has joined himself to the Lord say,
"The Lord will surely separate me from his people;"
and not let the eunuch say
"Behold, I am a dry tree."
For thus says the Lord:
"To the eunuchs who keep my sabbaths,
who choose the things that please me
and hold fast my covenant,
I will give within my house and within my walls
a monument and a name
better than sons and daughters;
I will give them an everlasting name which shall not be cut off.

Such a passage clearly reveals the sense of frustration and alienation felt by those within Israel who were foreign; were different. A homilist could explore this feeling of pain and alienation, with its accompanying depression, and could apply it concretely to real experiences in the contemporary world, including homosexuality. Thus a deeper sensitization of the parish community could take place.

2. John 8: 2-11

At daybreak he appeared in the Temple again; and as all the people came to him, he sat down and began to teach them.

The scribes and Pharisees brought a woman along who had been caught committing adultery; and making her stand there in full view of everybody, they said to Jesus, "Master, this woman was caught in the very act of committing adultery, and Moses has ordered us in the Law to condemn women like this to death by stoning. What have you to say?" They asked him this as a test, looking for something to use against him. But Jesus bent down and started writing on the ground with his finger. As they persisted with their question, he looked up and said, "If there is one of you who has not sinned, let him be the first to throw a stone at her." Then

> he bent down and wrote on the ground again. When they heard this they went away one by one, beginning with the eldest, until Jesus was left alone with the woman, who remained standing there. He looked up and said, "Woman, where are they? Has no one condemned you?" "No one, sir," she replied. "Neither do I condemn you," said Jesus, "go away and don't sin any more."

This parable of the adulterous woman reveals quite powerfully the tendency toward judgmentalism that exists within all of us. Each of us tends to magnify the faults of others, losing sight of our own weaknesses. Jesus' prescription to cast stones only when we are sinless reminds us that sinfulness is part of the human condition. Only God, who is good, has the right to judge us; and his judgment is one filled with mercy, not venom. A preacher explaining this passage could easily explore the ways in which we commonly cast the first stones of judgmentalism, including those cast against homosexual men and women because they are easy targets.

Preaching can be an extremely effective way of educating our people about the experiences of homosexual men and women, and we urge the priests and deacons of the Archdiocese to make a conscious effort to use homilies as one method of sensitizing people about the issues of homosexuality.

Education

The Church in the Archdiocese of San Francisco is blessed with an outstanding educational system. Through its schools, religious education programs, and youth activities, it brings the message and values of the Gospel to some seventy-five thousand young men and women each year. The schools and catechetical programs of the Archdiocese are a rich resource, and one which can give the Church a unique opportunity to assist in the value formation of our young people. Because of this, the Church has a special responsibility to educate young people about the issues of homosexuality: about the realities of a homosexual orientation, about the teachings of the Church, about the prejudice often directed against homosexual persons, and about the Gospel imperative to respect the human and civil rights of all people.

In assessing the efforts of schools in the Archdiocese to address this issue, we have been very impressed with the work that has been begun. Many schools have made a significant effort to sensitize their faculties and students to issues regarding homosexuality. Many high schools, in particular, have developed sound and effective curricula that explore the whole subject of homosexuality. We applaud these efforts, and we urge the schools of the Archdiocese to continue to formulate strong programs to treat this subject with openness and tolerance, while always being faithful to the full teachings of the Church.

Specifically, we urge all of the high schools in the Archdiocese to develop for implementation in the 1984-1985 school year a component for their mandatory curriculum that deals with homosexuality. This component could be part of a class on sexuality, or life-planning, or science. But whatever form this component takes, it should include the following elements:

a. Presentations on what the social sciences have revealed about the origins and nature of homosexuality;
b. Sessions dealing with the real-life experiences of homosexual men and women; their feelings of alienation, of depression, of being discriminated against, of whole personhood;
c. The teachings of the Church that homosexual activity is wrong, but that homosexual persons should suffer no prejudice or denial of rights, and
d. Discussions of the prejudices and attitudes that the students have toward homosexual persons and how they can be changed if they are negative.

Such elements in a high school program must, of course, be handled with sensitivity and care. But if our Catholic secondary schools are to be faithful to their mission of preparing men and women to live by Gospel values in our contemporary society, then their curricula must include some treatment of homosexuality.

In addition, the grammar schools and religious education programs of the Archdiocese should make efforts to foster in their students a full and deep respect for the human and civil rights of homosexual persons. Prejudicial attitudes are developed all too young in our society, and we have an obligation to work against intolerance at all ages. Thus teachers should be careful to deal effectively in their classes with any overt incidents of homophobia; and in teaching about the nature of Christian community, they should endeavor to promote respect for and acceptance of people of all sexual orientations.

CONCLUSIONS

In his recent pastoral journey to Central America (March 1983), Pope John Paul II urged all pastors in the Church "to preach with courage all the social implications of the Christian situation."

With this paper, the Senate of Priests hopes to follow this challenge regarding ministry to homosexual people, a ministry that seeks unity through harmony, a ministry that respects the diversity of gifts that are essential for the upbuilding of the common good of the Church.

The final canon in the newly promulgated *Code of Canon Law* tells us that always *(semper)*, the supreme law of the Church is the salvation of souls (c. 1752).

In all ministry to the homosexual person, this supreme law must be kept in mind. Pastoral ministry never seeks to minimize the normative teachings of the Church on the question of human sexuality. These normative teachings have been carefully explained in Archbishop Quinn's 1980 *Pastoral Letter on Homosexuality*.

Effective pastoral ministry always follows these normative teachings while reverencing the personal conscience of every individual. The struggle to assimilate well the meaning of one's homosexual orientation is never an easy task.

The oppression of sin enslaves us all and has created both personal and social isolation and division. Nevertheless, the "word of the Lord must speed on and triumph" (2 Thess. 3:1) and thus the Church must heal wherever there is a human person in need. We must reach out to those men and women authentically struggling with a homosexual orientation, and likewise call upon homosexual persons deeply to model their lives on the image of Jesus Christ.

We have rooted a good deal of the pastoral methodology of this paper in the principle of gradualism. We thus conclude on this same note, recalling the words of counsel of Pope John Paul II at the close of the 1980 Synod of Bishops that ". . . no one can do charity other than in truth . . . For truth is that which frees, truth is that which provides order, truth shows the way to holiness and justice.

It will never be enough, then, to accommodate oneself in a passive and easy manner to existing conditions and pressures, but we must consistently try with patience and good will to be ever more faithful in our whole persons to the duties and responsibilities of the Christian way of life.

We recall Pope Paul VI's Address to the International Congress of the *Equipes de Notre Dame* on 4 May 1970:

> "It is only little by little that the human being is able to order and integrate his multiple tendencies, to the point of arranging them harmoniously . . . This work of liberation, for that is what it is, is the fruit of the liberty of the children of God. Their conscience demands to be respected, educated and formed in an atmosphere of confidence and not of anguish. The moral laws, far from being inhumanly cold in an abstract objectivity, are there to guide . . . When (we) truly strive to live the profound demands of a holy love, patiently and humbly, without becoming discouraged by failures, then the moral laws . . . are no longer rejected as a hindrance, but recognized as a powerful help."

FOOTNOTES

1. *Pastoral Constitution on the Church in the Modern World,* 9-10.

2. The question of language is a complex yet critical one. For many people the term homosexual is neutral; for others it has distinctly negative implications. Many people view the term ''gay'' as the proper word to describe persons with a homosexual orientation; while others believe that gay implies support for the entire gay rights agenda. In determining a usage of language for this paper, we decided to follow the terminology outlined in *Homosexual Catholics: A New Primer for Discussion* (Dignity, Inc., 1980: "A Note on Word Usage"). This *Primer* indicates that the word homosexual includes all persons who are erotically attracted to members of the same sex. The word gay, according to the *Primer,* includes only those persons who have positively accepted this sexual identity. Since throughout this document we are speaking of those men and women who have a same-sexed erotic attraction, and not merely those who have positively accepted this sexual identity, we have consistently used the word homosexual. We have always used this word as an adjective in order to signal that homosexual persons should not be reduced merely to their sexual orientation, but rather enjoy a full and rich personhood.

3. See, for example, statistics published by Community United Against Violence, San Francisco.

4. The term "homosexual" is often used as if its meaning and connotations were self-evident. Footnote 2 addresses an example in terms of language that demonstrates that "homosexuality" is a very complex issue and does not admit of easy definitions. In terms of this paper, we consistenly mean by homosexuality the *orientation* of a person only and do not infer in any way that orientation automatically implies sexual activity. In light of this complex issue, we refer the reader to the article "Homosexuality" in the *Encyclopedia of Bioethics,* Warren T. Reich, ed., Vol. I, New York: The Free Press, 1978, 667-677. As used in this paper, therefore, homosexuality refers to a person's psychosexual structure and not to sexual activity.

5. See, for instance, the Statement prepared by Community United Against Violence, given to the Governor's Task Force on Civil Rights, 16 November 1981 (contact: CUAV, 514 Castro Street, San Francisco, 415/864-3112).

6. See, as example, John A. McHugh, O.P. and Charles J. Callan, O.P., *Moral Theology; A Complete Course, Based on St. Thomas Aquinas and the Best Modern Authorities,* Vol. I, New York: Joseph F. Wagner, Inc., 1958, p. 222, n. 621.

7. In n. 8 of the closing homily of the 1980 Synod of Bishops, the Pope made an important distinction between "a pedagogy, which takes into account a certain progression in accepting the plan of God, and doctrine proposed by the church, with all its consequences, in which the precept of living according to the same doctrine is contained; in which case there is not a question of a desire of keeping the law as merely an ideal to be achieved in the future, but rather of the mandate of Christ the Lord that difficulties constantly be overcome. Really, the 'process of gradualness,' as it is called, cannot be applied unless someone accepts divine law with a sincere heart and seeks those goods that are protected and promoted by the same law. Thus, the so-called *lex gradualitatis* (law of gradualness) or gradual progress cannot be the same as *gradualitas legis* (the gradualness of the law), as if there were in divine law various levels or forms of precept for various persons and conditions."

8. See Rudolph Schnackenburg, *The Moral Teaching of the New Testament,* New York; Herder and Herder, 1965 and Ceslaus Spicq, *Theologie Morale du Nouveau Testament,* 2 vols., Paris: Gabalda, 1965.

9. Such steps should include welcoming homosexual persons into lay ministries and onto parish boards and commissions. It is taken for granted, of course, that such people meet the same criteria as any Catholic in similar circumstances: i.e., holiness of life and faithfulness to the teachings of the Church.

10. See Reverend John F. Harvey, O.S.F.S., *A Spiritual Plan to Redirect One's Life,* Boston, Massachusetts, 1979.

Letter to Priests and Rationale for Welcoming the National Dignity Convention to Seattle

Archbishop Raymond Hunthausen
Seattle, Washington
June 8, 1983

Letter to Priests

Dear Father:

During the past many months, several national and local events, both within the public sector and the Church community, have given heightened visibility to the subject of homosexuality. As an example, only this week the National Catholic News Service reported three different stories, each of them dealing with a local Church (San Francisco and Miami here in our own country) and its response to the very challenging issue of how we as a Church community ought to relate pastorally to persons with a homosexual orientation.

Through all of this, one thing is becoming more and more apparent: homosexuality and the needs of persons with this orientation cannot and should not be ignored by the Christian community. Though the issue is an extremely delicate and sensitive one, we cannot let that stop us from dealing with it.

In doing so, we must be guided by the Church's teaching and by sound principles of pastoral theology. In addition, we can find help for our task in a growing body of knowledge and data being generated by social and behavioral sciences. But we need to realize from the start that whatever efforts we put forth will be misunderstood by many. A long history of ignorance, accumulated prejudice, and misunderstanding is not likely to be overcome at once. The fact, for instance, that persons with a homosexual orientation are often the objects of derision and ridicule in our society makes it difficult to find the kind of solid and rational ground that is necessary in order for a fair and reasoned dialogue on the subject to take place. But we must not let this deter us. In our mission as Church and in our role as pastors, we are called upon to provide the leadership, understanding, and compassion that are so often missing in our society's approach to controversial issues such as this one. If, in doing so, we sometimes run counter to that society's prejudices, we cannot let that deter us.

In my role as Archbishop, I share this pastoral repsonsibilty with you, and I am attempting to carry it out to the best of my ability. In recent months, for example, the Bishops of Washington State along with the Board and Staff of the Washington State Catholic Conference, have been struggling to address this very question. Our efforts have come to fruition in a statement you will receive this week from the Conference. The document strongly condemns prejudicial treatment and attitudes and affirms the Church's support of the civil rights of persons with a homosexual orientation. When you receive your copy of this document, I hope you will take time to read and study it.

On another level, I was approached by the local chapter of Dignity, an organization of Catholics with a homosexual orientation, and asked whether National Dignity would be welcome to hold its annual convention here in Seattle (September, 1983) and whether the closing liturgy of the convention could be celebrated in St. James Cathedral. After conferring with a representative group of your fellow priests, as well as with theologians and other advisors, I decided to grant this request. In doing so I was, of course, aware that some of our people might well question this decision or even misunderstand it entirely. This is a definite risk but it is one I am convinced we need to take as we attempt to deal with this delicate and highly-charged issue in a Christian manner.

I am hopeful that the enclosed statement which presents the thinking behind my decision to welcome the Dignity convention to this Archdiocese will help to answer questions you or your people may have, and that it will assist us in making this a "teachable moment" for our local Church.

As a further help to you, I am enclosing a far more thorough statement which deals with the issue of the Church's need to involve itself in an explicit ministry to homosexuals. It was developed three years ago by the Archdiocese of Baltimore and subsequently published in **Origins.** I believe that it outlines in a most responsible way a pastoral and theological rationale for ministry to the homosexual community. I commend the statement to you as well as its bibliography.

In closing, may I ask that you join with me in praying that we will be guided by the Spirit of Wisdom, Love and Compassion at this important moment in our life as a Church.

Raymond G. Hunthausen
Archbishop of Seattle

Rationale for Welcoming the National Dignity Convention to Seattle

Over the past few years, the official Church has begun to dialogue with members of the homosexual community and to minister in new and more open ways to persons with a homosexual orientation. There have been pastoral conferences on the east and west coasts and retreats for these persons. Some bishops have written pastoral statements on homosexuality and some have instituted special ministries to sexual minorities at the diocesan and parish levels.

I believe it is important to recognize that the Church's teaching on homosexuality has undergone development in recent years. We are coming to understand better the importance of distinguishing between homosexual orientation (the inclination of a person to be attracted to a person of the same sex) and homosexual acting out (the actual engagement in homosexual genital activity). As you well know, the Church's moral teaching opposes homosexual genital activity. It does not morally condem, however, or even criticize, homosexual orientation, because such orientation is not a matter of free choice and its causes are generally unknown. Given an understanding of this distinction, the Church states clearly that it is unjust and cruel to blame homosexuals for their orientation.

In their November, 1976 pastoral letter, *To Live in Christ Jesus,* the American bishops reflect this understanding and make a strong statement about the rights of homosexuals and the way our Church community should accept them. The bishops insist that "homosexuals, like everyone else, should not suffer from prejudice against their basic human rights. They have a right to respect, friendship and justice. They should have an active role in the Christian community." I consider this to be a very powerful statement, one that ought to guide us through our entire consideration of this matter.

Let me say, too, that a concern for justice for homosexual persons is not merely a theoretical concern. As Catholics and Christians we need to keep before our mind the fact that homosexuals are our brothers and sisters, made in the image and likeness of God. We are called to love and respect them as we are called to love and respect all of God's children. I think it needs to be said, too, that "those people" who will be gathering in Seattle for their convention and celebrating Mass in the Cathedral are really *our* people. Social science statistics generally place the number of homosexual persons at approximately ten percent of the population. This means that one out of every four families has a member with a homosexual orientation. Put another way, these statistics tell us that many of our parishoners have, or are related to persons who have, a homosexual orientation. They are part of our community and they need our pastoral ministry.

The question might still arise about the Dignity organization itself, and wether it is the best or most effective way for us a Church to engage in a ministry to persons with a homosexual orientation. I believe it is one good way and I also believe that our dialogue with and pastoral presence to the members of this organization will help us to discover yet other ways.

We are obviously in a process of discovery at this moment and I would be the last one to maintain that we have found the final answers. However, I am convinced that we will never discover the right answers unless we are willing th enter into dialogue with those who are struggling with the issue in terms of their Catholic faith. This is a big part of what Dignity is all about. Another aspect of this organization is the mutual support and challenge the members afford each other as they hear the Gospel message and attempt to follow Jesus. My experience with Dignity here locally tells me the organization is a significant help to its members in this regard.

In the final analysis, the measure of our pastoral care can, of course, only be the example of Jesus who time and again chose to minister directly to those whom society found most difficult to accept. As the enclosed article from *Origins* points out, Jesus not only reached out to these people, but he ''stood with them; he was one with them; he made their cause his own...The church, being faithful to Christ, continues his mission in its ministry...toward that end, it not only reaches out to help the poor, the powerless, the despised, but, as Christ did, it takes their part and makes their cause its own.'' It is in this spirit that I have told the Dignity organization that they will be welcome here.

Archbishop Addresses Issue of Homosexuality

Archbishop Raymond Hunthausen
Seattle, Washington
September 1, 1983

The following interview with Archbishop Raymond G. Hunthausen was conducted by Dr. Maury Sheridan, director of the Office of Communications.

Archbishop, the subject of homosexuality has received widespread attention publicly during the past several months. Is this subject a critical concern from the point of view of the church today?

Of course . . . any issue that is a source of human suffering—spiritual, emotional, psychological—is a central concern to the church. And homosexuality is such an issue.

There are those who would rather it were **not** a central concern. But wishing it so does not make it so, nor does it alleviate the human suffering.

For a long time, homosexuality was an issue we did not discuss. We knew next to nothing about it. During our seminary training we heard very little about it—except that it was "evil; a sin against nature," it was called. Like most of the material dealt with under the heading of sexuality, it was "not talked about."

By its very nature, homosexuality is a sensitive and volatile subject, fraught with misunderstanding and misinformation.

In dealing with the subject, where do we start?

Homosexuality is a complex issue. We need to begin by making the distinction, I think, between "homosexual orientation," the sexual attraction to a person of one's own sex, and "homosexual activity," the engagement in genital activity with a person of the same sex. It is acknowledged today that homosexual orientation is not a matter of one's free choice (any more than the color of one's eyes), and its causes are generally unknown. Obviously, I am not talking here about a **cultivated** homosexuality. Homosexual orientation does not automatically imply sexual activity. It is homosexual **activity** which presents a serious problem so far as the official teaching of the church is concerned.

What is the official teaching of the Catholic Church on homosexuality?

In general, the church teaches that a homosexual **orientation**, since it is not a matter of free choice, is morally neutral (not sinful), but that homosexual **activity** is objectively wrong (sinful).

In 1975, the Sacred Congregation for the Doctrine of the Faith issued the "Declaration on Certain Questions Concerning Sexual Ethics," and in 1976 the

American Catholic bishops published their pastoral letter "To Live in Christ Jesus."

The American Catholic bishops stated:

Homosexual activity . . . as distinguished from homosexual orientation, is morally wrong.

Pope John Paul II, in his remarks to the bishops in Chicago during his 1979 pastoral visit to the U.S., specifically confirmed this teaching.

The American bishops went on to indicate that some persons "through no fault of their own" have a homosexual orientation, and that:

Homosexuals, like everyone else, should not suffer from prejudice against their basic human rights. They have a right to respect, friendship and justice. They should have an active role in the Christian community.

The Vatican's declaration on sexual ethics also acknowledges that homosexuality can be an ''irreversible'' condition—the implication being that such persons are not morally blameworthy for such a sexual orientation.

Do you feel this "official position" on homosexuality is likely to change?

There are credible theologians in the church who say it cannot; there are also credible theologians who believe that it can. I am not a theologian, and so must leave speculative matters to those better qualified to deal with them. As bishop it is important for me to stand clearly with the tradition of the church on this matter.

As you intimate, there are contemporary theologians who are reexamining this position. What leads them to do so?

Let me start by saying it is important to recognize that certain aspects of the church's teaching on homosexuality have undergone development in recent years. We are coming to understand better, for instance, the important distinction between orientation and activity. The church, not unlike other institutions, draws from an increasing body of human knowledge in its reflection on the Word of God, which we call theology. An example of this is our understanding of Sacred Scripture which is constantly undergoing development that is in someways revolutionary.

Since "Divino Afflante Spiritu" of Pope Pius XII, no credible Catholic scripture scholar can be content with a literal or fundamentalist approach to the interpretation of Scripture on this or any other issue.

When one adds to this new developments in the human and behavioral sciences, it is not difficult to understand why theologians are continually involved in this kind of re-examination.

I must say I await with great interest the findings of our theologians and the ensuing dialogue between them and the church's Magisterium.

Why should the church be involved in this issue at all?

For a number of reasons, prominent among them the whole area of pastoral care. When Jesus was among us he ministered to all people in need, and the church can hardly do less today. Christ has called us to show compassion and love for one another. As Catholics and Christians we must keep in mind the fact that homosexuals are our brothers and sisters. We are all children of the same God, made in his image and likeness. We are members of the one Body of Christ.

Another reason is that while homosexuals are a minority group, they are a much larger minority than most of us are willing to admit. National statistics generally place the number at approximately 10 percent of the population. This means that one out of every four families has a member with a homosexual orientation. Put another way, these statistics tell us that significant numbers of our parishioners have, or are related to persons who have, a homosexual orientation. They are part of our community and they need our pastoral ministry.

Many of us ignore that fact. We set homosexual persons apart, label them as "different," and thereby target them for ridicule, scorn, injustice and even violence. Not surprisingly, many of these people have left the church. As the chief pastor of this church I want to do all I can to halt this exodus.

What do you have in mind?

We can begin by acknowledging that homosexual persons are a part of our Christian community—and for some of us this is painfully hard to do—and by ministering to them in compassionate and caring and, yes, challenging ways.

. . . and remember, when we speak of ministry to the homosexual person we must include in that ministry the families of homosexuals: parents, brothers and sisters, and spouses—many with homosexual orientations are married persons with families.

These family members have been almost totally ignored by the church. And they undergo intense suffering from anger, confusion and often deep-seated guilt.

Are you speaking of a ministry to the homosexual that is different from the ministry to the heterosexual?

The trouble with using terms like "homosexual" and "heterosexual" is that they limit the identification of the person to the sexual component alone. The other dimensions of the human personality are eclipsed, so that the other needs of the person—including the need for spiritual growth in faith—are overlooked or ignored. Ministry to all human persons must encompass the total being. Yet, we must acknowledge in our ministry to homosexuals the scorn, the isolation, they have come to experience by virtue of their orientation. They must be recognized as full members of the church, integrated into the parish community . . . and **that** is painfully hard for many of our people to accept.

What are some other characteristics of this kind of ministry?

Like all ministry, it needs to be modeled on the ministry of Jesus as we find it in the Gospels. It must be characterized by a spirit of healing and reconciliation. It must recognize that the homosexual person has a need for self worth, for love and a sense of community, for prayer and worship—in other words for a variety of ministers and ministries.

For example, our pastoral care must recognize the intense struggle that the homosexual faces and the challenge that our church presents in its call for chastity, a challenge that our divorced and other single Catholics know so well.

Always, of course, it must be carried out within the **normative** teaching of the church with relation to sexual morality. There are many more aspects of this kind of pastoral ministry than I have time to enumerate here.

What does the church draw from in developing a ministry to homosexuals?

Well, first of all the church draws on scriptural witness, its lived tradition, and sound principles of pastoral theology.

Pastoral theology has the benefit today of a growing body of knowledge acquired from the social, behavioral and physical sciences. Many responsible studies and a good deal of research and dialogue on these sensitive moral and pastoral concerns are taking place within our Catholic community.

In all of this, we need to be aware of the lived experience of homosexual persons and their families.

To this collective body of knowledge and experience we must bring openness of mind, critical judgment and a profound sense of charity—as well as a great deal of prayer.

Earlier you spoke of challenging the homosexual. What did you have in mind?

Maybe the best way I can respond to that is to share a quote from a pastoral statement on homosexual ministry developed by the Archdiocese of Baltimore (Feb. '82):

Homosexuals are called to the "same challenge that Christ has laid before all of us: 'Be perfect as your heavenly Father is perfect.' Not only must we demand from others respect for our dignity as human beings, we must live in such a way as to respect our own dignity. We must do justice to our personhood, for we have been created in the image and likeness of God.

Our response to Christ's call to perfection must be total, that is, it must be made at every level of who we are as persons. Heart and mind, body and spirit, all have to be developed and integrated to the fullest of our abilities . . .

With regard to our sexuality, this call to perfection is a call to form our lives according to the virtue of chastity . . . Through chastity we strive to live our sexuality to its human potential . . . This call to perfection through a life of chastity is addressed to all people, whether their orientation be heterosexual or homosexual, single or married.

I guess what all of this says to me, Maury, is that in one sense the Christian with a homosexual orientation is no different from any other Christian in the eyes of God or the church.

Turning to another matter, Archbishop . . . as a church leader, what kind of response to the growing dialogue on homosexuality do you expect from our Catholic community?

Educational Guidance in Human Love

Sacred Congregation for Catholic Education
Rome
November 1, 1983

Excerpt

Homosexuality, which impedes the person's acquisition of sexual maturity, whether from the individual point of view, or the inter-personal, is a problem which must be faced in all objectivity by the pupil and the educator when the case presents itself.

"Pastorally, these homosexuals must be received with understanding and supported in the hope of overcoming their personal difficulties and their social mal-adaption. Their culpability will be judged with prudence; but no pastoral method can be used which, holding that these acts conform to the condition of these persons, accord them a moral justification.

"According to the objective moral order, homosexual relations are acts deprived of their essential and indispensable rule".*

It will be the duty of the family and the teacher to seek first of all to identify the factors which drive toward homosexuality: to see if it is a question of physiological or psychological factors; if it be the result of a false education or of the lack of normal sexual evolution; if it comes from a contracted habit or from bad example;* or from other factors. More particularly, in seeking the causes of this disorder, the family and the teacher will have to take account of the elements of judgement proposed by the ecclesiastical Magisterium, and be served by the contribution which various disciplines can offer. One must, in fact, investigate elements of diverse order: lack of affection, immaturity, obsessive impulses, seduction, social isolation and other types of frustration, depravation in dress, license in shows and publications. In greater profundity lies the innate frailty of man and woman, the consequence of original sin; it can run to the loss of the sense of God and of man and woman and have its repercussions in the sphere of sexuality.

The causes having been sought and understood, the family and the teacher will offer an efficacious help in the process of integral growth: welcoming with understanding, creating a climate of hope, encouraging the emancipation of the individual and his or her growth in self-control, promoting an authentic moral force towards conversion to the love of God and neighbour, suggesting — if necessary — medical-psychological assistance from persons attentive to and respectful of the teaching of the Church.

* *The Human Person* (i.e., *Declaration on Certain Questions Concerning Sexual Ethics*)

Homosexuality and Human Dignity

Bishop Stanislaus Brzana
Ogdensburg, New York

January 5, 1984

Dear People of the Diocese of Ogdensburg
and of the North Country:

Homosexuality has become a serious problem in our country. Many individuals are troubled by feelings of homosexuality. Some openly admit to being homosexual and they call themselves "gay." They organize to protect their rights and to increase political influence. Some campaign to gain social approval of their "life-style." As a result, confusion has arisen in the minds of many and there is need for moral guidance. For this reason, I have decided to write this pastoral letter to present succinctly but clearly the teaching of the Catholic Church on this sensitive question, to guide people in the proper formation of conscience, and to show pastoral concern for those who are personally affected by homosexuality.

For the sake of simplicity of style, whenever the masculine pronoun is used in this pastoral letter it will include both sexes, except when it is clear from the context that only the male sex is intended.

Human Dignity

Before considering the moral and pastoral questions pertinent to homosexuality, it is important to put the whole discussion in its proper perspective. The starting point for the discussion must be emphasis on the inherent dignity of every human person, man and woman, created in the image and likeness of God. This dignity is greatly enhanced in baptism when we become followers of Jesus. St. Paul reminds us: "Are you not aware that you are the temple of God, and that the Spirit of God dwells in you? If anyone destroys God's temple, God will destroy him. For the temple of God is holy, and you are that temple" (I Cor. 3:16-17). This dignity pertains not only to the spiritual part of man — his soul, but also to the physical part — his body. For this reason, St. Paul further states: "You must know that your body is a temple of the Holy Spirit, who is within — the Spirit you have received from God. You are not your own. You have been purchased, and at a price. So glorify God in your body" (I Cor. 6:19-20). Therefore, since we are persons of such high dignity, we must live and act in accord with that dignity.

I would be naive if I did not acknowledge that the subject is sensititve and volatile. And I would be less than honest if I did not admit that the responses will vary, depending upon the level of understanding.

The topic of homosexuality - within the context of sexuality in general - is no longer a "closet" issue among Catholics. They are certainly in touch with the world in which they live and are exposed to the tremendous media coverage that the issue has been given, both seriously and superficially. Catholics are as well informed as other segments of society, and I believe they are as capable of open and reasoned dialogue on contemporary moral issues.

This is not to say that some of the dialogue will not be marked by heated emotions, hostility, fear and lack of knowledge.

Those are painful risks we take if we are to grow in our faith. And with that pain will come deeper understanding, compassion and a fuller awareness of what Christ has called us to . . .

Archbishop, could we focus for a few moments on the Dignity organization which will have its national convention here in Seattle this coming weekend?

Well, as you know, Dignity is an organization of Catholics of homosexual orientation. To understand the group we need to reflect on a few things . . .

It can hardly be denied that the homosexual in the Catholic community has been the recipient of misunderstanding and prejudice. Because of this, most of these people have felt unwelcome in our parish communities and many have drifted away.

It would be naive to think, then, that these people would not seek out some support group or organization in order to gain some healing and relief from their isolation and loneliness - out of desperation, if nothing else. And certainly to seek dialogue with the church. This is especially true of the Catholic who recognizes his or her need for spiritual development.

It was an awareness of these kinds of needs that prompted me to tell the leadership of Dignity that they were welcome to hold their convention in this archdiocese. Over the past years, the official church has begun to dialogue with members of the homosexual community and to minister in new and more open ways to persons with homosexual orientation.

I must admit my own knowledge of Dignity is limited. I have not had extensive contact with the organization. It is young, and as with any organization, I'm sure, its members do not speak nor think with one accord. I would like to make it clear that my welcome to the Dignity organization does not mean I embrace the position of each and every member of Dignity. I do hope that their presence among us will add to our church's dialogue with the homosexual community and help us minister to them in new and effective ways.

One final question: There are some within our Catholic community who are disturbed that the Cathedral will be used by the Dignity organization for a liturgy during the convention.

I am certainly aware that some of our people are concerned - perhaps that's too mild a word - about this. One thing about being a bishop, you are continually faced with issues that bring pain to someone . . . that cannot prevent a bishop from acting or from addressing controversial issues.

These people, these "other people" are **our** people. As I have said, they too are members of the Body of Christ. They have the same need for the sacraments as the rest of us. We have no right to deny them the use of our church. To do so would be to judge their standing before God.

When I was approached by the local Dignity chapter and asked whether the closing liturgy of the convention could be celebrated in St. James Cathedral, which is within walking distance of the convention hotel, I conferred with a representative group of my fellow priests, as well as with theologians and other advisors. On the basis of that consultation, I granted the request, even though I realize that some of our people might well question the decision or even misunderstand it entirely. I decided that this was a risk that ought to be taken in order to deal with this delicate and highly-charged issue in a Christian manner.

Thank you, Archbishop.

Homosexuality in General

Homosexuality is a psychosexual orientation or attraction toward persons of the same sex. When it occurs between women it is also called Lesbianism. Generally speaking, a person does not choose to become homosexual. Rather, at a certain point in life he discovers that he is homosexual.

Experts are not agreed on the causes of homosexuality. They propose various theories: heredity; lack of healthy family life, weakness or absence of the father, or a dominant mother; inadequate education; lack of effective peer relationships; arrested emotional development; lack of normal sexual development; narcissism, and others. It may be that homosexuality results not from one factor alone, but from a combination of factors, congenital and acquired.

Homosexual Attraction versus Homosexual Acts

Homosexual attraction itself, although a deviation from the normal instinct of nature, is not sinful. However, a person who is affected by homosexuality has the responsibility to take steps to overcome it or, at least, to hold it in check. This is similar to the responsibility of heterosexuals who must control their sexual instinct, and must avoid doing what is wrong.

It is a different story, however, with external acts of homosexuality. Such acts, according to the constant and firm teaching of the Church, are seriously wrong. When committed with sufficient reflection and freedom of the will, they constitute grave or mortal sins.

That homosexual acts are wrong is shown by natural law. God, the Creator of nature, established sexual attraction between men and women in order to unite them in marriage and allow them to express mutual love and to bring forth children. Thus human sex has a unitive meaning and purpose and a procreative meaning and purpose. Homosexual acts are contrary to both.

From what has been stated above, it is clear that marriage can exist only between man and woman. So called "marriage" or partnership between two persons of the same sex for the purpose of homosexual activity is perverse and seriously wrong.

The Testimony of Sacred Scripture

The prohibition of natural law against homosexual activity is confirmed in Sacred Scripture. We are familiar with the history of the cities of Sodom and Gomorrah in the Old Testament (Gen.19:1-19). God destroyed both cities because of the immorality of their citizens, particularly because of homosexual practices. The majority of the Fathers of the Church support this interpretation. The very word "sodomy" in our language, meaning unnatural copulation, is taken from the name of the city of Sodom. In the Book of Leviticus we have the precept: "You shall not lie with a male as with a woman; such a thing is an abomination" (Lev. 18:22; see also Lev. 20:13).

The Old Testament prohibition against homosexual activity is continued in the New Testament. In his letter to the Romans (1:18-32), St. Paul declares that all men must be able to recognize the existence of God from the works of creation. Those who refuse to do so are not excused. Their hearts are darkened, and God allows them to fall into immoral practices, including homosexual behavior. St. Paul also states: "God therefore delivered them up to disgraceful passions. Their women exchanged natural intercourse for unnatural, and the men gave up natural intercourse with women and burned with lust for one another. Men did shameful things with men, and thus received in their own persons the penalty for their perversity" (Rom. 1:26-27). In his letter to the Corinthians St. Paul states bluntly: "Do not deceive yourselves: no fornicators, idolaters, or adulterers, no sodomites, thieves, misers, or drunkards, no slanderers or robbers will inherit God's kingdom" (I Cor. 6:9-10).

Declarations of the Magisterium

Responding to the problem of homosexuality, the Bishops of the United States have given testimony to the constant and firm tradition of the Church in the following public documents: *Principles to Guide Confessors in Questions of Homosexuality,* issued in 1973; and *To Live in Christ Jesus* (p. 19), issued in 1976. In 1975 the Sacred Congregation for the Doctrine of the Faith issued a *Declaration on Certain Questions Concerning Sexual Ethics* in which it states: ". . . homosexual acts are intrinsically disordered and can in no case by approved of" (n.8).

Rights of Homosexuals

As stated before, gay people sometimes demonstrate for their rights. They indeed possess rights, not because they are homosexuals, but because they are human beings and members of the Church. Their rights should be honored despite their homosexuality.

However, it is often evident that while campaigning for their "rights" gay people are really striving to gain social approval of their "style of life," including homosexual activity. Such approval cannot be granted. On this point God has clearly spoken in Sacred Scripture, and the Church, in fidelity to truth, continues to echo his words. In *A Pastoral Letter on Homosexuality*, issued May 5, 1980, Archbishop John R. Quinn of San Francisco states: "The claim that homosexuality is simply a variant of normal sexual behavior and exists alongside heterosexuality as an equivalent expression of adult sexual maturation must be rejected." Hence, what is wrong remains wrong and cannot be made right either by Gallop Poll or public ballot, or by government edict.

Exhortation to Homosexuals

I now address my words to those people of our diocese and our area who are homosexual. Despite all problems, I remind you that you remain children of God for whom Christ died and for whom the Church has genuine concern. I ask you to keep in mind your great dignity as sons and daughters of God in whom His Spirit wishes to dwell as in a temple. Seek spiritual and professional counselling in order to overcome homosexuality, if possible, or at least to hold it in check. Pray constantly to God for help. Turn frequently to the Sacrament of Penance and Holy Eucharist for spiritual strength. Follow the challenging example of the Saints who, despite many temptations, excelled in purity and chasity. Pray to Mary, the Immaculate Mother of God. With determination and courage, and with the abundant help of God your difficulties can be overcome or, at least, can be controlled.

Pastoral Care of Homosexuals

We are all sinners and the Church extends to us God's mercy and forgiveness in her sacraments and shows pastoral care in many other ways. Those who are afflicted with homosexuality are entitled to the same pastoral care. This care is extended with understanding, compassion, and sensitivity, but without permissiveness. The purpose of such care is to turn homosexuals away from error and sin, to lead them to truth and virtue, and to bring them and keep them close to God, who calls us ". . . from darkness into his marvelous light" (I Peter 2:9).

Conclusion

Jesus tell us: "I have come to call sinners, not the self-righteous" (Mark 2:17). Aware of our own sins, we must have charity and compassion toward all our neighbors, our fellow-sinners, among whom there may be some homosexuals. We must pray for them, and help them. At the same time we must form our consciences correctly, according to the truth, and advise others correctly.

God's great gift of sex must be used properly, according to His plan. Its abuse will turn us away from God; its proper use in marriage will draw us closer to God. We must worship and serve God not only with our spiritual faculties, with our soul, but also with our physical faculties, with our body. That is why St. Paul reminds us: "You are not your own. You have been purchased, and at a price. So glorify God in your body" (I Cor. 6:19-20).

Asking the Lord to bless you all abundantly, I remain

Fraternally yours in Christ,
Most Rev. Stanislaus J. Brzana, S.T.D.
Bishop of Ogdensburg

Letter on Homosexuality

Archbishop James A. Hickey
Washington, D.C.

April 5, 1984

Dear readers of the Catholic Standard, my brothers and sisters in Christ,

In discussions about homosexuality, as in all other questions that touch our lives as Catholics, we need to hear the genuine teaching of the Church. For that reason I have asked the Editor to highlight some excerpts from recent official teaching which can assist you in reading and evaluating the articles and discussions found in this issue.

Homosexuality is a topic frequently misunderstood, enormously complex and charged with much emotion. It has many implications for the family and political life of our country. By "homosexuality" I mean a predominant, persistent and exclusive pyschological attraction toward persons of the same sex. This attraction is often referred to as a "homosexual orientation." It must be distinguished from sexual acts with persons of the same sex. This behavior is called "homosexual activity." Confusion arises when in certain writings and legal references the term "homosexual orientation" is used to describe not only the attraction but also the activity. We must make this distinction, however, in order to understand the teaching of the Church.

In recent years, objections have been raised against the Church's condemnation of homosexual acts. These objections appeal to new scientific discoveries, to a different way of understanding the teaching of Sacred Scripture, and to the influences which ignorance, prejudice and social conditions might have had in determining the Church's teaching. The Church has taken into account all these objections and has given clear guidance regarding homosexuality.

In 1975 the Sacred Congregation for the Doctrine of the Faith issued a statement entitled *Declaration on Certain Questions Concerning Sexual Ethics*. It presents the teaching of the Church on homosexuality clearly and with pastoral concern. In 1976 the bishops of the United States treated the same subject in an important section of their pastoral letter, *To Live in Christ Jesus*. Pope John Paul II addressed this question in remarks to the bishops at Chicago in 1979. On November 1, 1983, the Sacred Congregation for Catholic Education, under the direction of Cardinal Baum, restated the Church's teaching on homosexuality with clarity, insight and pastoral understanding in its instruction on sex education, *Educational Guidance in Human Love*. These sources present an authentic body of Catholic teaching, written in view of present circumstances, based on the Holy Scriptures and the constant teaching of the Church.

These documents of our Church point out that a homosexual orientation is not morally wrong in and of itself. Those who experience this orientation are not to be maligned. Instead they are to be helped through positive and sensitive pastoral care to live lives of true chastity in the power of the Holy Spirit. At the same time, the Church teaches that deliberate homosexual desires and acts are gravely evil. They are a disordered use of the sexual faculty given us by God.

All of us must offer one another support in leading chaste lives. All of us are called to chastity whether homosexual or heterosexual. Homosexuals are harmed, not helped, when we condone or appear to condone what is called "a homosexual life-style." This phrase refers to everything which fosters or even glorifies homosexual activity as an alternative to marriage, a chaste single life, or consecrated celibacy. These ways of life are in agreement with the inner logic of our nature; to one of them each of us is called by Christ. Sexual intercourse when practiced between persons of the same sex is not consistent with our human and Christian vocation. Once that truth is understood, we can make solid progress in the pastoral service of homosexuals.

Various organizations of Catholics claim to offer support to homosexuals. Their worth must be measured by their clear and unequivocal acceptance of the Church's teaching on homosexuality. They must not place homosexuals in situations in which there is real danger of serious sin. Only then can they be truly effective in providing support for homosexuals to live prayerful Christian lives, with complete abstinence from all sexual activity.

In general, I believe it is a mistake to isolate homosexuals from the rest of the faith community. Spiritual support groups should be aware of this danger. We worship God as believers in Jesus who accept His word and Sacraments, and who acknowledge together our sinfulness and beg His merciful pardon. All of us must be prepared to take up our cross daily and follow Christ. There is no other Name by which we can be saved, except that of Jesus.

To live in Christ Jesus requires above all that we be people of prayer. Everyone, homosexual or heterosexual, must see prayer as the sustaining life-blood of our spiritual existence. As Catholics we have the immense support of the Sacraments of the Church. The Sacrament of Penance offers powerful assistance, a remedy in weakness, and a release from the sin for which we are truly sorry. This realization is very important for the homosexual as well as for all of us who are struggling to live a life in conformity with Christ's law. Freed from sin by a worthy reception of Penance, each member of the Church community has the strength, nourishment and consolation of the Blessed Eucharist, the Body and Blood of Jesus Christ. He comes to help us on our pilgram way.

Our homosexual brothers and sisters deserve good pastoral care based on the teaching of the Church. Our parishes need to be signs of Christ's love, forgiveness and truth. We need to examine our attitudes and practices to dispel ignorance, discrimination or insensitivity. Homosexuals can profit from and should receive adequate counseling and, when necessary, psychological help. We must reach out to their parents, to offer them support and guidance. Pastoral care should also be provided to the husbands and wives of homosexuals. We must minister in truth but likewise serve with love and compassion.

While the Church believes homosexual activity is clearly wrong, the Church also believes that all persons, including homosexuals, are entitled to their basic human rights. No one, of course, has unlimited rights. Each of us must respect the rights of others. Hence it is unjust when homosexuals are deprived of their basic rights as a result of prejudice or discrimination. Legislation to secure those rights must be written with care, not only to protect individual persons, but also to avoid the legitimation of a homosexual life-style or a legal equivalence between homosexual activity and that marriage between man and woman which is the foundation of family life and the cornerstone of our society.

I call on all our priests and people to reflect the teaching of the Church in their lives and in their service to homosexual men and women. Rather than establish a new office or special ministry of the Archdiocese, I shall seek to foster a concerned outreach to homosexuals in our parishes, neither isolating nor separating them from the parish communities. Those who genuinely and clearly accept the teaching of the Church and offer programs in full accordance with that teaching shall have my encouragement. Those who deny the teaching of the Church or equivocate by offering alternatives to official Church teaching must know that I am obliged by my duty as bishop to refuse both recognition and support.

My friends, this letter has not attempted to touch all the ramifications of this subject. I wished merely to present with clarity the teaching of the Church and to ask your continued prayers for our homosexual brothers and sisters who with great earnestness and generosity seek to follow the way of Christ. Let us serve them in truth and Christian love.

Sincerely in Christ,

James A. Hickey
Archbishop of Washington

Statement of Massachusetts Catholic Bishops

Bishops Daniel Cronin, Timothy J. Harrington,
Bernard F. Law, Joseph F. Maguire
Boston, Massachusetts

May 31, 1984

At the present time, there is a bill before the General Court of Massachusetts seeking "the elimination of certain discrimination on the basis of sexual preference."

During the past few months, the Massachusetts Catholic Conference has been asked to articulate its position on this issue. These requests have come not only from legislators who are seeking guidance from us on the Church's stance but also from concerned members of the Catholic Community who feel that the lack of an official statement on this question implies a shift in our position concerning the morality of homosexual activity.

Conscious of our role as moral leaders in the community, we, the Roman Catholic Bishops of Massachusetts have decided to explain the position of the Catholic Church on this matter. We do so because the proposed bill has power to influence the lives of the youth as well as the adults of our Commonwealth and because it has grave implications for the common good of our society.

First of all, some comments are in order on our Church's stand on the question of homosexuality. Contemporary scholars make an important distinction between homosexual orientation (psycho-sexual attraction primarily directed toward members of the same sex) and homosexual activity (homogenital acts.) Such orientation is regarded generally as morally neutral; it is viewed as a condition which, through no fault of the person involved, implies a lack of complete sexual integration. *Homosexual activity,* on the other hand, is seen as something *objectively wrong* inasmuch as it falls short of the ultimate norm of Christian morality in the area of genital expression, i.e. a relationship between male and female within the marital union. Whether or not homosexual activity is *subjectively wrong* (sinful) will, as in all human actions, depend on the presence of those elements of knowledge and freedom constituting the human act.

Secondly, some comments are also in order on the phenomenon known as discrimination. It must be remembered always that there is a necessary distinction, very often ignored, between unjust discrimination (the arbitrary limitaion of human rights) and the necessary limitation placed on the exercise of human rights whenever such actions would interfere with the just rights of others and harm society. All people of good will must oppose unjust discrimination. However, there are times in our lives when each of us experiences the pain, discomfort and challenges of necessary limitations on our rights whenever there is a prudent judgment that the common good is at stake. For example, having a patient in an ambulance does not permit the driver of that vehicle to ignore pedestrians at a crowded intersection. Homosexuals, surely, possess all the rights proper to human beings but, as in the case of heterosexuals, these rights should be limited whenever they come into conflict with the rights of others and the common good.

As the Roman Catholic Bishops of Massachusetts, we firmly oppose all forms of unjust discrimination whether against homosexuals or heterosexuals. We are of one mind and one heart with the sentiments expressed by the Catholic Bishops of the United States in their pastoral letter on moral values *To Live in Christ Jesus* issued in November, 1976: ''Some persons find themselves through no fault of their own to have a homosexual orientation. Homosexuals, like everyone else, should not suffer from prejudice against their basic human rights. They have a right to respect, friendship and justice.''

In reply to those who have requested our opinion of the bill presently before the legislature, we now wish to present some serious pastoral concerns which will place us among those members of the Commonwealth who oppose its passage.

First, experience has shown that the passage of legislation of this type will be seen by many as a step toward legal approval of the homosexual lifestyle. Our concern in this regard is heightened by a common perception in our country that whatever is declared legal, by that very fact, becomes morally right. The tragic abortion experience of the past ten years in the United States bears out the necessity for caution in these matters. Thus, our failure to oppose this bill could give rise to the false impression that the Catholic Church accepts the homosexual lifestyle as a morally feasible option.

Secondly, the Catholic Church, in her hiring practice is obliged to reflect her stance on the morality of sexual activity. She has the right and the duty to establish certain standards of conduct for everyone she employs. If the Church favors this bill as it stands, it is quite possible that an improper interpretation of it may be advanced in the future, denying hiring discretion whenever legitimate questions arise about the appearance, lifestyle and activity of certain homosexual employees.

In voicing our opposition to the passage of this bill, we must state publicly our disapproval of the unjust harassment of homosexuals by members of the heterosexual community. Such behavior is unconscionable and it must be stopped. However, we are of the opinion that this will be achieved only by a process of consciousness raising leading heterosexuals to proper respect for persons who happen to be homosexuals. What we need is education and a change of heart, not new and ill-advised legislation.

Such are our prayerful and heartfelt concerns about the passage of this bill. For the reasons stated above, we do not favor its approval by our legislature.

We do not deny that some members of our Church have homosexual orientation. There is room in our Church for everyone. Homosexuals, too, are our brothers and sisters in the Lord.

Our decision to stand in opposition to the passage of this bill must not be seen, therefore, as indifference to the serious difficulties experienced by people who are homosexuals. Even though we take a firm moral stance on this issue and have many questions about the legitimacy of homosexual lifestyle, we urge proper respect for the rights of every citizen of the Commonwealth. We will do all in our power to dispel the unfortunate myths and misunderstandings related to this issue. Finally, we stand in opposition to every form of harassment and unjust discrimination directed against homosexuals and we respect them fully as fellow pilgrims on our earthly journey toward the Kingdom of God.

Letter on Violence to Archdiocesan Deans

Archbishop John R. Quinn
San Francisco, California
August 2, 1984

I am writing this letter to you and to the other Deans in the Archdiocese in light of the increasing violence against homosexual persons.

I ask you to communicate to the priests and those who collaborate with them in roles of leadership and responsibility the utter incompatibility of such acts of violence with a witness to the Gospel. Nothing can justify these attacks on homosexual persons and the Church must clearly repudiate all such acts.

Violence is not the way of the Gospel. Violence is not the way of the Church. Violence is not the way of Christ.

Our role as priests is a difficult one. We must be faithful to the moral teaching of the Church concerning homosexual acts. At the same time we must unfailingly have the compassion and kindness of Christ in our pastoral service. Thus we know and experience the constant tension between our role as teacher and our role as pastor. The difficulty, of course, lies in being faithful to both. But that is what we are called to and we must draw strength not from our own human resources but from the Lord who strengthens our weakness by His power.

We live in times when there is much evil, malice, injustice and hate. But let us never forget that we also live in times when there is much goodness, heroism and unselfishness. We should encourage our people to be tireless in building an earthly city in which justice, truth, holiness and peace reign. As believers in the Gospel, we must live not only by faith. We must also live in unshakable hope. It is not enough for us to condemn violence. We have the arduous task also of building up humanity in justice, dignity and freedom according to the plan of God who sent His only Son not to condemn the world but to save it, not to announce death but to announce life.

Concern First for People

Archbishop John F. Whealon
Hartford, Connecticut

July 13, 1984

Recently in Hartford, as in New York, San Francisco and other major cities, a public demonstration was made by homosexual or gay people. Since 1974 there has been a growing public affirmation by individuals of their own homosexuality. There have been pressures to end prejudicial attitudes towards homosexuals in housing, hiring practices, teaching opportunities, etc. And there have been growing pressures for recognition of the homosexual lifestyle as legitimate and worthy of societal, legal and ecclesiastical approval.

In view of this, an explanation of Catholic teaching concerning homosexual people and homosexuality is timely. But this is a complex question indeed.

The Church is concerned first of all with people. How people are classified is secondary, and is intended merely to help towards understanding people. Unfortunately some classifications have judgmental connotations. It is regrettable that the term ''homosexual'' tends to classify people principally by their sexuality. The Church must see all people, irrespective of their sexuality, as children of God and destined for eternal life, as deserving of human understanding and love.

The homosexual is defined as a person to whom people of the same sex are more attractive than those of the opposite sex. But to limit this attraction to physical and even just sexual attraction is a misleading generalization. Close friendships between persons of the same sex may be completely free of erotic or sexual behavior.

The number of homosexual people is difficult, if not impossible, to determine. Reasonable estimates suggest that between four and five percent of the total population are exclusively homosexual. This is a notable percentage. Fewer women than men reportedly are homosexual. But a further problem is that people cannot be categorized as simply heterosexual or homosexual. Studies indicate that very few people are totally masculine or totally feminine. In people in whom heterosexual disposition is dominant, there seems to be a latent potentiality for homosexual interest which the person may not suspect. Some people can go through a homosexual phase of their lives.

The causes of homosexuality are many, and no one can be isolated. Heredity as a cause has never been proven convincingly. Environment, upbringing, emotional relationships within the family, an over-dominant or possessive mother and a weak or absent father — all these and similar factors are presented as possible explanations. But there is no agreed opinion. The causes of homosexuality are a mystery to us.

The basic distinction in discussing this question is between homosexuality as a condition, and homosexuality as expressed in genital activity with a person of the same sex. The Church teaches clearly that genital activity by God's plan is for the basic purpose of procreating the human race. Therefore genital activity by unmarried persons, or by married persons without being open to procreation, is morally wrong and presumably sinful. For people who are not married, heterosexual or homosexual, the chastity of the unmarried is the Christian moral obligation.

Without compromising its biblical and traditional moral teaching, the Catholic Church in general and the Archdiocese of Hartford in particular need to reach out with pastoral care for homosexual sons and daughters. They have a particular cross to carry through life. The consciousness of being "different," of belonging to a minority, of being handicapped, leaves the homosexual person suffering from the same problems as all minority and handicapped groups, with the added factor that their "difference" is usually secret. This leads to a deeper alienation, a greater loneliness.

In a society that can see them as objects of cruel jokes and contempt, homosexuals may suffer from a lack of self-esteem and an isolation that heterosexuals find difficult, if not impossible, to comprehend. Homosexuals can feel like strangers in ordinary mixed society. They can be shunned and rejected by people who may have an inaccurate or distorted knowledge of the homosexual person.

We are learning to treat the handicapped not with pity but with respect, with an awareness that often through their handicap they can reach a degree of compassion, self-giving and sanctity which is denied to people not similarly afflicted. The promise to homosexuals in Isaiah 56:4-5 needs to be heard and known by them. They need to know the Church's loving care and service.

Letter to Illinois Gay and Lesbian Task Force

Cardinal Joseph L. Bernardin
Chicago, Illinois
January 2, 1985

Excerpt

Let me state clearly at the outset that I am not afraid to take an unpopular position in defense of human or civil rights. However, I know you understand that any leadership I might provide in regard to such issues would have to be exercised within the parameters of the Catholic Church's teaching. That is simply my responsibility as a bishop.

I would first like to clarify the Catholic Church's position about homosexuality and gay/lesbian rights. Basically, the church's mission is to proclaim Jesus Christ and his Gospel. Our values and understanding of the basic dignity of *every* human person — including gays and lesbians — are based on this. More specifically, four principles shape our teaching about homosexuality and gay/lesbian rights:

1) Some people, through no fault of their own, find themselves to have a homosexual *orientation*. This orientation is *not* in itself immoral or sinful. This is why the Catholic Bishops' 1976 pastoral letter, *The Gift of Sexuality (sic),* states: "Homosexuals, like everyone else, should not suffer from prejudice against their basic human rights. They have a right to respect, friendship and justice. They should have an active role in the Christian community."

2) There is no place for arbitrary discrimination and prejudice against a person because of sexual attraction. We especially deplore violence and harassment directed against such persons. Moreover, all human persons, including those with homosexual orientation, have a right to decent employment and housing.

3) However, homosexual *activity*, as distinguished from homosexual orientation, *is* morally wrong. A corollary of this traditional teaching of the Church is that patterns of life, sometimes referred to as "life-styles," which encourage immoral behavior are also morally objectionable. I agree with your assertion that there is a wide spectrum of gay and lesbian life-styles. As a Church, we do not approve of those patterns of life or lifestyles which encourage, promote, or advocate homosexual activity.

4) Parents have the right to keep their children free during their formative years of any person(s) or influence(s) which might draw them toward homosexual practice or condoning homosexual activity.

Let me expand on this last point. We do not assume that many homosexuals are child abusers or seducers of young people. We have not recommended the firing of any persons of homosexual orientation from Church-related positions where they may be simply disliked. Moreover, we do not ask questions about sexual orientation in our Archdiocesan hiring procedures. Of course, any employee of a Church-related institution acting in a non-professional manner on the job or seeking to teach in a way contrary to Catholic morality would be subject to disciplinary action. That would include anyone who promotes or advocates a *heterosexual* lifestyle which we would consider immoral, as, for example, people living together without the benefit of marriage.

My own position, then, is this: I firmly deplore acts of violence, degradation, discrimination, or diminishment of any human person — including anyone with a homosexual orientation. I am especially concerned that such attitudes or acts might be found at times in institutions of this Archdiocese. At the same time, as a bishop in the Catholic Church, I am equally bound to teach that homosexual activity and patterns of life which promote it are immoral.

My specific concern about gay rights legislation is its implications. If it implies acceptance or approval of homosexual activity *or* advocacy of a lifestyle which encourages homosexual activity, we will have no choice as a Church but to oppose the legislation. If if merely provides needed legal protection for people with a homosexual orientation and *explicitly* does not approve homosexual activity or endorse the kind of lifestyle which would promote it, we could support it.

As I stated above, defending civil rights and supporting specific legislation are two separate issues for me. To provide leadership with regard to either of them, I must be faithful to the office I have accepted in the Church. This means, in part, exercising with fidelity my teaching role as a bishop.